MW00651102

Surrender

A journey towards a fulfilled life

Shannon Jamail, M.S.

 Scooter Publishing
California

2018 Scooter Publishing Inc.

© Copyright 2018 by Scooter Publishing Inc. and Mind and Body Complete Inc.

Published in the United States by Scooter Publishing Inc., California.

Library of Congress Catalog-In-Publication Data
Jamail, Shannon

Surrender: a journey towards a fulfilled life / Shannon Jamail

Library of Congress Control Number: 2018905109
ISBN 978-0-9817789-8-3

Edited by Amelia Travis, stokedyogi.com

Printed in the United States of America

Author photo on cover: Sarah Reid
Cover image: Pixabay, Creative Commons CC0

scooterpublishing.com

Surrender

/səˈrendər/

verb

cease resistance

may you always feel & choose love! ♡

Praise for Surrender

"This book is a mind-changer, game-changer, and if you let it be, a life-changer. Shannon gets to the heart of it and doesn't shy away from sharing her own messy, imperfect, sometimes WTF stories that ultimately, make you realize you're not alone navigating the complex world of your own mind. Reading this book gave me inspiration and permission to examine my own judgement, fear, limiting beliefs, control issues, and a bunch of other junk but here's the cool thing: it helped me unpack these gremlins and look at them with eyes of love. I highly recommend this book for any human on their journey of self-awareness who wants to laugh, cry, and maybe cuss a little on their way to a more fulfilled life. I will be gifting this book to all my friends who are ready to outgrow their bullsh*t thought patterns and blossom into hilarious, sassy and more enlightened versions of themselves. Read it! You'll be glad you did."
- **Amelia Travis**, Business Entrepreneur, Coach, Editor and All Around Kickass Momma

"I am so touched by Shannon's words in her book, Surrender. Her real life examples are very relatable. Her processing of her own stories is therapy for the reader. This is written so thoughtfully - to have lasting impact!"
- **Sara Dean**, Speaker, Writer, Podcaster, and a Beautifully Shameless Mom

"Through Shannon's book, Surrender, we feel her journey to success- earned through perseverance in times of pain, anxiety and fear which provides us an opportunity for introspection on our own limiting beliefs. Her thought-provoking stories and insights offer a valuable perspective of healing and hope for us all. Shannon's authentic approach to life will inspire you to live each day to the fullest. This is a must read for anyone wanting to expand and grow!"
- **Mary Cafarelli**, Human Resources Professional and a Light Shiner

"After reading Shannon's book, I realized that we all have internal struggles that we contend with on our quest for peace and self improvement. It is apparent in Shannon's personal stories and thoughts that she cares about the work she does and approaches everything in an unselfish way with the goal of helping others- and that is what this book will do- help others. This book reminds us that it is ok to be vulnerable and real. No matter your experience or how you label yourself- you can rejoice in the fact that it will be a blessing to read this book and experience wisdom and guidance that can transform your life! This book will inspire you to be the best version of yourself as it has done for me!"
- **Kristalynn Nisbet**, Business Owner, Entrepreneur, Gorgeous Momma of 6 and Grandma of 2

"It is evident that Shannon has done that deep-down-soul work. Her words are honest, brave, raw and authentic. Shannon is graciously casting light on familiar shadows, leaving the reader feeling a sense of connection and safety. If you're looking for a space to feel accepted and worthy with a gentle reminder that 'you are not alone' - this is it."
- **Dee Mullin**, Certified Professional Sales/Leadership Coach & Spiritual Badass

"A life-changing read for anyone ready to take control of their world, through awareness, intent, and damn hard work. Shannon shows up in her book as raw, authentic and completely honest. She invites the readers into her journey to Surrender and the realization that, "I am enough". She provides the reader with space to assess without judgement, reflect without regret and the ability to create a life full of love. Life is sometimes messy, sometimes painful, always a beautiful gift, and always our choice to live fully no matter the circumstances. A MUST READ."
- **Ruth Nelson**, Corporate Executive and Fellow Wine Connoisseur

"Shannon has such a beautiful way of getting to the heart of a topic, bringing life to it, and then offering practical applications that are not only doable, but effective at yielding change. This book emulates Shannon's zeal for life and leads you into meaningful connection within yourself and the people you love and surround yourself with daily."
- **Becky Branch**, Licensed Clinical Therapist & Beautiful Soul Sister

"This is the most thought provoking book I have ever read. It really made me think about things I have done for years that we're not only tearing myself down, but gave off a toxic environment for those around me. It's honest and simple, yet goes right for the heart. I learned that I am in control of my own happiness. It's all in retraining your brain on how you see things. It's so empowering! I wish I had read this book a long time ago!"
- **Sue Thomas**, Family Medicine Practitioner and a Take No Bulls*t Go Getter

"A powerful guide that will aid you in shifting your thinking to new heights of love & fulfillment! An absolute must read!"
- **April Parker**, Real Estate Guru and Best Mommy Mentor

"We're all navigating towards our truth, our authenticity and our purpose. In this book, Shannon delivers perspective and truth with practical steps on how to arrive at being your best and most authentic self. With sass and candor, she shares practical steps on how to motivate yourself with positive self-talk, and honestly access how your thoughts and actions become your reality. You can change your brain, mood, attitude and the energy you surround yourself with. The book delivers personal reflection and stories paired with practical steps on how to accomplish joy, peace and passion. Shannon delivers with truth and honesty. I recommend reading for anyone who wants to create change in their lives, lasting change."
- **Angel Murr**, Designer and Fellow Lover of All Things Beautiful

Dedication

This book is dedicated to you. May you find light within these pages. May you recognize the beauty, strength and power within you. May you feel loved.

With Gratitude

First, my soulmate. There has been one person in my corner, regardless of my mood, temperament, job title (or lack thereof), health, hair color or shopping habits — my best friend, my husband. Nathan, I cannot find the words to express the depth of the love and appreciation I have for you. Thank you for always fighting for us, thank you for always loving me, and thank you for being our light.

My kids all deserve special awards. Awards for putting up with my 'ugly mom moments', temper tantrums and my selfish nature. I would not be the person I am today without each of you in my life. I am not perfect, and never will be, but please trust that my love for you *is* perfect and that, without hesitation I would give my life for yours. And possibly go to jail for you. Depends on the circumstances, so let's maybe not test that one out.

In the process of editing this book, my editor asked me where I learned to love so fully. My answer came without hesitation or a second thought: "My aunt and my nonna."

To my aunt Theresa who took me in, no questions asked and loved me completely; who has shown up in my life, every day, since my birth, without wanting anything in return except love; who showers my children and my husband with untethered, beautiful sacrificial love: Thank you, thank you, thank you.

To my Nonna, who showed me what it was like to love others through food, grace and strength: I can't wait to sing and dance with you in heaven.

To my editor Amelia — what can I say? You believed in this book. You believed in me. You helped bring my thoughts to life in the most moving way. I am forever grateful you took a chance with me.

Thank you to the many people who have contributed to raising me: my biological parents, from whom I learned how to work hard and to never let anyone or anything hold you down. My step mother, from whom I learned to face obstacles with a strength I never knew I had. To my many 'adoptive' parents, including friends who took me off the streets, aunts, grandparents — thank you for reaching into your hearts for a girl who was too full of shit to know better. To my in-laws, who have shown me what it looks like to show up, thank you for loving me and *all* of my kids unconditionally. Thank you all for doing so much for me- I hope you know that you are loved.

To family, friends and clients who shower me with affection, even when I don't deserve it, who support me, encourage me and love me in so many ways: I can't name you all, but hopefully I show and tell you and you can feel that you are part of my tribe.

Table of Contents

Introduction

Without suffering, we have no growth or expansion. Without pain, we are oblivious to love and compassion. Without these dark places, we can become self centered, sad for unknown reasons, and unfulfilled. Yet, when we are in the hell of suffering, the darkness of it, the pain of it- we tell ourselves to *escape*. The mind wails, races, gnashes its teeth and clamors for us to get out, avoid it, to numb the pain any way we can. We are so very afraid of it.

This was me: Always in fear, anxious for known and unknown reasons, and oblivious to the real needs of myself, let alone anyone else. I was self centered in an obnoxious, unproductive way. Hiding from the truth, I became a liar. I worried that I wasn't enough, then worried that I was too much.

I ran from pain and suffering in unhealthy and unproductive ways. In so doing, I was unknowingly blocking abundance and love.

New Orleans, 2013'ish: After completing a residency for school in which I was challenged in more ways than I would want to ever admit, I, for unknown reasons, suddenly found myself in a disturbing, shaky and unsettling place. Things were beginning to awaken inside of me that I didn't really want to mess with. Awareness stirred, and new consciousness began to rise from the depths within me, changing my vision and perception of self, giving me new eyes to see my shortcomings. I was starting to recognize the judgment and ugly criticism in me. Despite appearing to be a giving and loving person, my generosity and kindness were shrouding a self centered need. My external appearances did little to reflect the *comparison, gossip, self doubt, insecurity* and *anxiety* that were inwardly eating me up and spitting me out.

I was being attacked, consumed by forces which raged inside me — a battle invisible to outsiders, but creating absolute devastation within. In the midst of this suffering, I found myself on my knees crying out for help with my whole heart. In the throes of my anguish, I shouted at God, at the Universe, "I can't do this anymore!" In desperate prayer, I pleaded for an answer to my internal madness. "Please, help me escape this noise and suffering," I begged, "Deliver me from this pain."

Ask and receive. I got an answer.

Surrender.
Trust.
Align.
Choose Love.

I didn't know this was my answer at the time. At least I couldn't articulate it. It wasn't a voice booming down from the heavens. It wasn't a sign conveniently written on a post it note. It was a knowing which rose up within me — a still, small voice, which sounded remarkably like my own. It was a blossoming of truth from the center of my own being.

Surrender.
Trust.
Align.
Choose Love.

I didn't hear it, didn't see it... I *felt* it. Each step, one at a time, unfolded into my consciousness and settled comfortably into place, like it knew right where it needed to be, like it was coming home. These steps, so clear in my heart, revealed themselves to me with the certitude of unshakable truth, and have become a stronghold and refuge when the clamors of darkness, fear, anxiety and judgement arise.

On every journey, the first step is the hardest. Yet it resonated within me as the one which mattered most: *Surrender*. I knew that my perceived control, my resistance to suffering, to learn and grow and change - this was only creating more suffering. I knew, in that instant, that I had to surrender control.

This books takes you on my journey- which, by the way, isn't done yet. The steps that have taken me from a place of pain and anxiety to a place of love and freedom. There isn't a miracle in these pages, other than the miracle of my journey and awakening.

There also aren't any bad guys in this story. I am not a bad guy despite my mistakes and actions, nor is anyone else. Any suffering experienced in here is a blessing of growth, of transformation. Without it I wouldn't be who I am today, and I am proud of who I am and who I am becoming.

I almost didn't write this book... for years. For many reasons. Because I didn't think I was good enough. Or bad enough. Or tragic enough. Because I wasn't creative enough. Because I worried I would hurt people. Because I worried my truth would look different than someone else's truth. Because I worried that people from my past would read this and think, "Uh, who is she trying to be? I know that ghetto ass girl, and this isn't the language she was speaking back in the day."

All of this is true. All of this is false. It's true only in that I believed it once. It's false because I no longer do. One of my all time favorite quotes, from the late, great Maya Angelou: "I do my best until I know better, then I do better."

My entire life, I was doing my best, even if it was destructive, hurtful or hateful. Just as *everyone* is. We are all doing the best we can with the tools we have and the life experiences we have thus far lived.

I am also not an expert on anything but myself (and barely that.) No amount of degrees or certifications can make one an expert, despite today's western cultural norms. This is something that's taken me two degrees and hundreds of certifications to realize. No matter how educated I am, it's impossible for me to be an expert on you, or you to be an expert on me. There are billions of neurons within us and around us. Each one affects each of us in different ways, and they cross over, change, adapt, grow and die.

This book isn't written to be an expert guide, road map, or a magic wand. It is merely an invitation to expand. Whatever doesn't feel right, let it go. Whatever doesn't align with you — surrender it in love.

Welcome. Inhale deeply my intention for everything good, and release fully any expectations or judgements. May you read this book with your heart wide open, and may the truth that you need wash over you.

I love you.

> *Success isn't measured by what you have, but by how often you are aligned in love.* - **Shannon Jamail**

Note to reader: At the end of each chapter you will find a prayer or ask of the universe. Feel free to take a few quiet moments to center yourself. Close your eyes. Breath deeply a few times and then recite the prayer (or make one of your own).

This book is designed to help you gain insight and take positive action. Reflection questions are provided at the end of each chapter to help you implement the tools provided. Feel free to answer them directly, or just free write. Grab your favorite journal, set a timer for 4-7 minutes and just write, without stopping, everything that comes to mind from each chapter.

PART 1

Surrender

Ego

> *We must go beyond the constant clamor of ego, beyond the tools of logic and reason, to the still, calm place within us: the realm of the soul.*
> - **Deepak Chopra**

The sun was high, radiating an oppressive, tangible heat, which made it difficult to move, breathe, or even think. It was aggressively hot — like, not normal hot, but the kind of hot I'd imagine the first step into hell would be. Maybe the second step. Shit... how many steps to hell are there?

Never mind. It was all of those steps, a sweltering obsidian staircase descending to the molten core of the earth. Sweat poured off my brow, dripped into my eyes and down my face, beading on my upper lip. Every lick of it made me dizzy with thirst. I labored over each breath as dust from the dry, cracked earth swirled around me. Like a strange combination of sloth and tortoise, I harnessed all of my energy to slowly hoist and drag each foot off the ground and place it one pathetic inch in front of the other. Maybe it was more than an inch. Maybe it was not even an inch.

The heat was like a thick, wet, wool blanket on my back that I was dragging with me: itchy, wet, steaming, and heavy. So, so heavy. Stubborn and determined, I refused to look up and see what was ahead of me, and instead kept my gaze down, staring blankly at my dirt-covered shoes as I inched them forward toward my destination. Blinking through the sweat in my vision, I stole a side glance at my husband. He was staring at me with a terrible look, a combination of fear and horror. It was the kind of look you reserve for a dog that was just struck by a vehicle, and you're waiting to see if the dog will get up and walk away or just lie there, lifeless, defeated, and broken. I could see in his eyes, and feel radiating from him, a palpable fear that his wife was just a few steps away from being roadkill.

People were passing without pause on the other side of me. My God, one was jogging. *These people can kiss my sweltering, sunburnt wet ass. Wait. That is not right. I am so happy for them. I celebrate them. Whatever.*

My husbands lips were moving soundlessly from the landscape of his inquisitive gaze. He asked me something, I think. Maybe he asked if I was ok, or if I'd like to sit down, or if he can carry my camel back, or if I'd like to grab a pitcher of margaritas.

"Yes, margaritas," fell out of my mouth, the words stumbling drunkenly across my overheated, clumsy tongue.

"What?" he said.

"Nothing," I mumbled.

"I think we should stop," came clearly to me from his lips.

"No," I said. "No."

Despite my delirium, there was a stubborn bitch inside me who refused to quit. Thanks to her, and some unfathomable combination of miracles, we dragged ourselves like grime-covered zombies across the finish line.

It was an obstacle race, only six miles, if memory serves. Maybe it was twenty. It sure as hell felt like twenty. My ego was crushed in this race. Six years prior, I might have run it. Well, maybe not run it, but accomplished it with a measure of grace and strength now impossible, save for my memories. Six years prior, my husband wouldn't have stared at me the entire race, wondering if at any moment he was going to have to carry my ass or call for a stretcher.

But that was six years ago... that was before. This is now. And now, today, comes with different blessings, in all shapes and forms, sometimes even disguised as illnesses. And still, I show up. I am really, really good at showing up. It is my thing. Showing up, I dare say, is my super power.

My super power, like many super powers, however, is tied to my ego.

Ego isn't *always* bad. Or at least the power that can be harnessed from it can be used for good. It can keep us focused on our goals, motivate and inspire us to accomplish what we set out to do. It can be the cattle prod that nudges a person to finish a Spartan race in the middle of a fucking desert and triple digit heat, gaining them kudos and pride despite the lack of shade and an overwhelming personal aversion to the solar rays which attack one's body and immune system like a bloody terrorist.

Ego, the great (and sometimes sadistic) motivator.

Ego can be a cheerleader in your head, saying, "Yasssss, keep going! You are on the right track! Don't give up! You got this!"

Ego can also be a total jerk. "What are you, a wimp? You said you were going to do this, so do it. Are you going to let that girl beat you? You are worthless."

Ego is sometimes the star quarterback of the mind's small-town high school; self-obsessed, vain and conceited. With swagger and bravado, it parades itself around in it's varsity letter jacket, singing it's own praises: "I am the bomb, I am better than everyone. I am so good at this thing — NO, everything! Just look around. All these losers are below me".

Freud referenced the ego as "a man on horseback, who has to hold in check the superior strength of the horse."

Ego, when harnessed by our inner spirit, champions and encourages, reminds us of our strength and virtue, and inspires us to rise to the occasion, preaching, "You have the ability to heal yourself and others. You can accomplish these goals, and help your tribe accomplish theirs."

Much of what I have read teaches that ego is completely bad, that ego is our enemy. There's even a book I love called *Ego Is The Enemy* by Ryan Holiday. In one of my favorite texts, *A Course in Miracles*, the author frequently uses the word ego to denote wrong-mindedness, while right-mindedness is considered the domain of the Holy Spirit.

Despite these teachings, I don't believe ego is the entire enemy: I believe we have the power of choice. Our response to ego can make it an enemy, but it also has the potential to be a powerful ally. The trick is to ask yourself: Am I using the power of ego for good, or for self-sabotage?

Reflecting upon that sweltering, torturous, delirium-inducing adventure race, I can't help but question my motives. How much of my motivation was rooted in showing off, proving my abilities and worth to others? Was I driven by narcissism and bragging rights?

Did I finish the race to prove to myself I could do it, or did I finish it so I could tell other people I did?

At the end of the day, what's the difference?

Intent is the difference. Intent is what determines if the experience helps us grow, or keeps us small. Ego participates with our inner spirit. This inner spirit takes the clamoring of our ego and determines if the intent is for our highest good, or for lowly, selfish purposes and, ideally, harnesses the power of the ego for our highest good.

Ego can also easily be confused with identity. One of my favorite psychoanalytic fathers, Carl Jung, asserted that the ego represents the conscious mind as it comprises the thoughts, memories, and emotions of which a person is aware. He believed the ego is largely responsible for feelings of identity and continuity.

When I chose to leave my lucrative, luxurious, well-respected corporate gig and become self employed, my pseudo ego suffered a definitive bruise. My concept of self was shaken. My identity was inextricably tied with my professional self, and deciding to make my own way in the world meant I found myself uprooted, untethered, and searching to reclaim my place in the world. Who was I, if not an executive at a Fortune 500 company, with over seventy five employees reporting to me and a multimillion dollar budget? Inwardly, I wondered if I'd reduced myself to nothing more than a one stop shop, begging for business.

This identity struggle continued for quite some time, and I found myself engaged in a battle between my ego and inner spirit. Ego (the asshole) was taunting me, baiting me with snide remarks and self-reproach. Like a catty girlfriend giving a back handed compliment, it whispered, "You are so much better than this, what are you doing?" It reminded me pointedly, and often, about the dwindling status of my savings account, the designer shoes I was no longer buying, and the prestige I used to flaunt, now fading into a worn patina on a decade old luxury sedan.

Somewhere below ego's constant pestering was a still small voice, speaking words of a peaceful warrior directly to my heart. With firm compassion and unwavering grace, it spoke through the doubt and fear, reminded me of my intention, and lifted me up in love. "This is your passion, your dream, your purpose," inner spirit said. "Don't stop. Don't give up. Don't look back. Move into it. Keep going."

Buoyed by the voice of my highest self, I kept putting one foot in front of the other, moving slowly and steadily toward the life I'd envisioned.

The battled waged on, and eventually my inner spirit won over my ego. I realized I'd been comparing apples and oranges. The corporate life, despite its perks and privileges, was at that time, not right for me and my aspirations. Freedom was the path I made for myself, even if it meant an arduous trek across unknown landscapes. The road less traveled was the road for me. With patience, and let's not lie, some tears, bruised knees and wine, I eventually harnessed the power to say, "I am so much better than wallowing in self doubt. I've only got one life to live, and, I'm going to give it my all. Let's do this!"

It should be noted that the battle between ego and inner spirit isn't won once and for all. It rages on, day after day, week after week, month after month, year after year. The secret weapon in winning the battle is learning how to discern the voices of ego versus spirit.

That's the hard part; sifting through the mind chatter and discerning the truth of the heart. What message do we listen to? Which voice is talking? How do we know we are aligned with good intention?

How do we ensure we are operating from a place of hope and love instead of ego and fear?

Signs you are operating from a fear and ego-based place:

» When you make important decisions, your main goal is to avoid pain, discomfort and confrontation.

» You make knee jerk reactions that at first bring you relief, then in reflection cause anxiety, fear or worry.

» You seek accolades and recognition from others.

» Making decisions feels difficult for you without confirmation from other people.

» You feel physically uncomfortable in your stomach and chest when making decisions or acting on ideas.

These social and somatic cues indicate a disconnect between intuition and actions. I am continually astonished at the intelligence and complexity of the human body and brain. We are hard wired with powerful intuition, a gift that can be honed and sharpened with intentional practice.

Here are the steps I take to make sure I am intuitively making decisions via my inner spirit instead of acting based on ego's need for approval:

» **Ask yourself questions.** Inquire within about the issue, thoughts, or behaviors on which you need clarity, and see how your body reacts. Our bodies are extremely tuned into the intelligence available to us, and can act as a tuning fork or gauge for true feelings. Experiencing bodily pressure, discomfort or pain when we consider issues, thoughts, or behaviors is a strong indicator that we are not operating for our highest good. Simplify this, and ask yourself a yes or no question to something you are trying to decide. When you think about each response, which feels right? Not easy, necessarily, but right in the deep sense of knowing. Keep in mind, sometimes a healthy fear is relevant when we are being pushed outside our comfort zone, but will also include a good dose of excitement to balance it out and still feel right.

» **Meditate. Breathe. Go inside.** We tend to have racing thoughts surrounding decisions, opinions and judgments. Listening to your inner spirit is damn near impossible if it is not quiet enough to hear and feel the responses. Countless books have been written on meditation, but it doesn't have to be complex. Here are two ways you can find more clarity amongst a rowdy mental landscape.

A. *Simple breath counting technique:* Breathe in to a slow count of five. Exhale to a slow count of five. Repeat this at least 5 times. You'll notice the mind chatter begin to slow, allowing you more clarity to feel and hear your inner spirit.

B. *Mindful moment:* Take a period of time, anywhere from one to thirty minutes, and check in with your five senses. Notice what you feel physically, what you smell, what you see in this moment, what can you taste, and what sounds you hear? Observe your senses without judgement (as much as possible.) If thoughts arise, and they will, simply note them ("ah, I'm planning again", "Oh, there's my old friend worry"), and then let them go, like clouds in a clearing sky. Allow all your senses to extend outwards, not attaching to anything, but allowing them to simply wash over you.

» **Ask a trusted tribe member.** This is not the same as feeling indecisive and asking for opinions in order to make everyone else happy. Rather, checking in with a trusted friend, partner coach, or counselor can help you confirm that the place you are coming from isn't rooted in fear, jealousy, anger, spitefulness, or bitterness. There is great value in community, in acting as mirrors for one another. Seeking dialogue with a trusted tribe member who wants the best for you and others can help you clear any resistance or blocks, and help you consider perspectives you may not be able to see on your own.

» **If all else fails, stop.** If you are still unsure, take a break, a nap, sleep on it. When in doubt, stop, and rest.

My prayer/ask of the universe:

Please guide my heart, open my mind and harness the power of my ego to my inner spirit. Help me to operate in the highest power of my intuition. Allow me to use my voice and my actions to serve a higher good for myself, and those I love.

Questions to ponder:

What was the last decision you made that felt like an inner spirit guided you?

_____

_____

_____

Consider how your body felt, how your heart was beating, what your stomach felt like, what thoughts were occurring. What are some signs that your inner spirit is guiding you?

_____

_____

_____

Fear

> *You gain strength, courage, and confidence by every experience in which you really stop to look fear in the face.* - **Eleanor Roosevelt**

I used to have an intense, debilitating, overwhelming fear of flying. I'm talking the kind of fear which prompted me to pop some Xanax, drink a glass or three of overpriced mediocre wine in the airport bar, and make a concerted effort to walk a straight line down the jetway before pouring myself into a seat on the plane, thereafter mostly unconscious for the duration of the flight.

Needless to say, this wasn't a fun, let's party kind of intoxication. It was an — I need to shut out the world, inebriated so I don't crumble inward from the weight of my terror and panic — sort of deal. Public service announcement: Don't do this if you can help it, it's kinda really dangerous. I do not endorse or advocate this kind of behavior. Can you imagine if there'd been an emergency? I would have been completely unable to function.

Immediately after flying, I would invariably text my closest friends something like this:

"Mother f'er that flight was HORRIBLE. It was SO bumpy, I am pretty sure the wing broke during the flight and the captain crapped himself... or possibly that was me."

When I didn't take anxiety meds, I cried uncontrollably. I'm talking sobbing, choking, can't catch my breath, people are staring kind of episodes. I also found myself inexplicably angry when I didn't pop some pills: mad at myself for being afraid, mad that the plane had duct tape on the window, mad at the weather, mad without cause, rhyme, or reason; just mad.

If I didn't take the medication (which I hated, by the way, because of the terrible headache after), I drank, heavily and to the point of near stupor, no matter what time of day it was. It could have been a 6am flight and you'd better believe you would have found me glued to a barstool, boozing my way into fearlessness. If you don't yet have the picture, let me phrase it this way: I wanted to change my state of mind so dramatically that if, God forbid, the plane were to crash, I wouldn't give a damn, but be singing and dancing (or blissfully unconscious) as my sky taxi plummeted to certain doom.

Around the year 2000, I worked in corporate America and traveled constantly as part of my job. The fear of flying, and subsequent self-numbing, were weekly occurrences in my high pressure, high power gig. It shames me now to admit that when the horrific tragedy of 9/11 happened, my flying fears were validated and I found a selfish silver lining.

"This is my solution!" I thought. "Now I can use the fear of terrorists to tell my boss I can't fly." I did just that, and surprisingly they accepted it and allowed me to take a train for about a year.

During that time period, I had also planned an incredible trip to Jamaica with a group of friends. Our itinerary was mapped out, and I was looking forward to a week of sand, sun, and umbrella-cocktails with some fun loving gals. Yet fear found a way in and did what it does best, paralyzed me. My gripping flying terror crippled me into denying myself what would have surely been a beautiful adventure.

Several weeks before we were to leave for Jamaica, I started having recurring nightmares and vivid waking visions of dying on the flight. Every time I thought about the trip, instead of feeling joy and excitement, I became frozen with fear. It got so bad, I went to a doctor and requested a note which explained that due to anxiety, I would be unable to fly. I used the note to cancel the trip for a full refund, which left the rest of the group disappointed, and resulted in me missing an awesome experience.

When we allow fear to run the show, it runs rampant and merciless through our minds and prevents us from showing up how we're meant to. When we give fear the foothold, we grant it permission to steal our joy and rob us of incredible life experiences.

Fear doesn't always show up as nail-biting, goose-bumping jumpiness. It's insidious and creative. Fear can sneakily disguise itself in other emotions like anger, pain, bitterness, anxiety or hate. Consider the basis of past arguments in which you've participated, or those you have witnessed. What looks like an angry fight on the surface is often an exchange of fears: fear or being hurt, rejected, disrespected, or unloved. Aggression presents an offense so that fear can stay safely coiled inside, doing what it does best: preventing us from showing up and shining.

Fear keeps us small. How, then, can we overcome fear? Is that even possible?

Let's get one thing straight right now. We cannot get *rid* of fear. Don't misunderstand me — the goal is not to abolish fear, but to embrace it. Fear exists for a reason, to be a protective force guiding us away from things which may harm us. The purpose of fear is to, via intuition, steer us away from threats to our precious lives.

Believe it or not, fear can be looked at lovingly. Fear is a mother bear protecting her cub. When imminent danger is present, whether real or perceived, fear propels us into the necessary fight or flight state which will arm us against the adversary, or equip us to flee with haste. Fear, in itself, is not bad. It is our reaction to fear that determines whether it will result in good or bad, help or harm. Our response and relationship with fear can alter our lives for better or worse.

Signs you may be allowing fear to rule:

» You envision rejection, failure, or even catastrophe when planning something new.

» Your self talk sounds something like this: I cannot do that, they won't like me, that is not my strength, I am terrible at, there is no way that I can achieve that, I'm going to fail.

» You physically get ill, or shaken, when approaching experiences outside of your comfort zone.

» You think chasing dreams is something other people do (or an unattainable fantasy).

» You are waiting for someone else to confirm your decisions, thoughts, or plans.

» You feel physically uncomfortable in your stomach and chest when making decisions or acting on ideas.

Most of my life, at least for as long as I can remember, I have struggled with debilitating anxiety (see also the chapter on anxiety and stress). Not the type of anxiety of a little excess worry, but the kind that paralyzes, leaving me frozen, unable to move, think, or decide. I'm talking about palpable, tangible, all consuming, soul-crushing anxiety. Picture racing heart, breathless, elephant on my chest, sweaty palms, inability to swallow, full on meltdown, panic mode shutdown kind of anxiety.

Sometimes this anxiety has a trigger, like flying. Sometimes it is just there, unprovoked and uninvited. Some nights I go to bed happy as a clam, only to wake up feeling sick with dread, a heaviness unrelated to any specific thought, feeling, event or situation.

Sometimes the anxiety feeds and fixates on seemingly trivial "what-if" scenarios. What if what I said to a friend may have hurt her feelings and now she won't like me as much? What if I said the wrong thing yesterday during the bar-b-que? Cue the slew of physical and mental anguish. My anxiety chases it's tail tirelessly, until I finally get pissed off and recognize the cycle of madness taking place.

Other times anxiety hones in on catastrophe instead, painting elaborate mental pictures of a myriad of horrors. I might envision my family being killed in some horrible but totally possible way, and then I can't breathe, or move, or think. On other occasions, social anxiety rears it's ugly head and whispers slippery and stifling accusations to me, convincing me that I just can't put my social face on this day. It tells me everyone will see through it, that I won't be funny enough, educated enough, outgoing enough — just not enough, period. It whispers until I cancel, call in sick or reschedule, keeping me captive in isolation until the 'real and tougher' version of me can come out of hiding. Anxiety holds me in bondage until my higher self, the one unfettered by the heaviness of my fears, puts her party pants on and shows back up.

Today, I still struggle with anxiety and wrestle with fear, but I show up anyway. I embrace the discomfort, greet anxiety like an old friend, and rise to the occasion. I do what I am afraid to do and let my actions fly in the face of my fears.

In Rory Vaden's book, *Take the Stairs*, he tells a story of a woman so overcome with fear of confined spaces that she hid under her desk during a fire, choosing to die instead of going out through the fire escape. *That is how strong our fears can be.* Thankfully, a firefighter found her, paralyzed by fear, and encouraged her to make her way to safety with him. Her face was tear-streaked and contorted with anguish. "I can't," she said, "I am too afraid."

"Do it anyway," the firefighter replied. "Do it afraid."

Do it anyway. Do it afraid.

My eight year old daughter is not my adventurous one. The wild child is my six year old, who will literally jump off of a cliff, just for the fun of it. My eight year old, on the other hand, wouldn't jump off the cliff even if she was strapped to the strongest cable and completely enclosed in a protective bubble. No way, no how, no jump, no risk.

During a Christmas break a couple years ago, we took a detour coming home from visiting Texas and stopped at White Sands National Park in New Mexico. This magnificent park is one of the most amazing places I have ever been to. Picture miles and miles of beautiful white sands, stretching out as far as the eye can see, in the middle of nowhere. Vast, glistening white hills of sand without end in sight. It's remarkable.

Anyhow, we purchased sleds — the hip thing to do — and went on a search for the tallest most amazing hill we could find to sled down. At the top of our first hill, my six year old jumped on her sled and took off before I could even tell her to hold on. Sure enough, moments later she went flying one way, the sled the other, laughing her little butt off as she tumbled away. My eight year old, on the other hand, was adamant and tearful in her refusal to get on the sled.

"I can't do it mommy." she cried, trembling in fear with tears streaming down her sweet face.

"Why?" I asked her.

"I'm afraid!" she said, visibly shaking.

"Let's do it anyway, baby," I told her. "Let's do it afraid."

Lo and behold, she did. She did it afraid. Arriving at the bottom of the hill, her previously terrified expression was replaced with a glorious, incredulous, self-satisfied joy. It lit up her face and she shone, beautiful, bright, and bold.

That is how we do fear. We do it anyway. We do it afraid. And when we do, the breathtaking joy, transformation, and strength on the other end is life changing.

How to show up and do it afraid:

» **Use the power of your thoughts and words.** When it came to flying, I went through conscious and intentional reprogramming in order to, today, get on a plane without medication or alcohol and fly comfortably. For me, this is like running two marathons back to back — a big f'ing deal. I changed my words from "I am afraid to fly" to "I know flying allows me to experience amazing things". The words you choose to express fear are important and powerful. Choose empowering words, not fear based words.

» **Understand that fear is not the enemy.** This may sound cheesy, but thank your fear. Be grateful that your body, your protective system, is in place and wants you safe. Change your mindset from "fear is my enemy blocking me at every turn" to "fear is my protector when I need it" to take the power away from your fears and into your hands.

» **Don't fight with your fear.** Don't beat yourself up. Don't berate yourself, the fear, or the situation. Be open and gracious. Ask yourself, "What can I learn from this fear? What is it trying to tell me about me? How can I view this in love?"

» **Do it afraid.** Don't limit your potential because of fear. Unless it is something that will negatively impact your life, or causes you undue actual risk, then do it. Do the thing you are afraid of. Do it anyway. Do it afraid.

My prayer/ask of the universe:

Thank you for the intended protection of my fears. Allow me to embrace my fear and to show up anyhow, heart forward, ready to learn and love through it. Thank you for the lessons, the growth and the strength I continuously gain by showing up through my fears.

Questions to ponder:

Think to one of the most fearful times in your life and you showed up anyhow. What did you learn?

_____

_____

_____

What are you going to do today to show up despite your fear?

_____

_____

_____

Judgment

> *Real magic in relationships means an absence of judgment of others.*
> - **Wayne Dyer**

Last year I spent a weekend at a yoga ashram. For over a year, I'd been searching intently for a place to spend time in quiet reflection. My hope was to find a space designed to facilitate deep healing and introspection, a safe and sacred space which would allow me to simply rest in the stillness of my own being.

I was having a hell of a time finding a place that spoke to me. Though I routinely hold space for women around the country in retreat formats myself, and despite my familiarity with what makes a safe and healing space, I found it surprisingly difficult to find what I was looking for. In fact, I struggled to even articulate what I was seeking. I felt what I was searching for, but I was hard pressed to put it into words, much less get Google to understand the nuances of my quest.

In time, I gave up and released it to the universe. Originally disgruntled and disappointed, I said forget it and gave up looking, then took a moment to say silently; the right place will find me when I am ready and released it with ease. Not surprisingly, once I surrendered, the perfect place landed right in my lap, through no conscious effort of my own. A beautiful mentor and friend told me about a quiet, remote healing destination set on a spacious farm in Northern California, the Sivananda Yoga Ashram. Upon navigating to the ashram website, I felt a deep pull and calling to go there. There were no flashing signs or neon lights, no magical computer voodoo, just a deep knowing that resonated within me.

"Yes," the knowing said, "you'll find your quiet here. It's serendipity and synchronicity. It's exactly what you need. This is the place."

The universe was conspiring with me in gracious manifestation of my blessings. Not only was the ashram the right place for me, but my mentor called me back and casually mentioned that she happened to have a credit which would just cover the tuition for the very weekend I hoped to attend, and she wanted to give it to me as a gift. When the divine has a will, it will surely provide a way. This was a surefire sign that I'd found the right place. Encouraged and inspired, I packed my bags and mala beads, put on my game face for some woo-woo shit, and off I went, a happy hippie on her way to a new adventure.

My goal in retreating to the ashram was to turn within and find peace. It often feels as though my whole existence has been wrapped up in turmoil, anxiousness, anger, fear and worry. I can boldly claim this truth: I am a master worrier. Like, I have awards for it... in my head anyhow. For this weekend retreat, my goal was to meditate, pray and seek ease within. I wanted silence. I wanted quiet reflection.

I. Wanted. Peace.

Here is the thing with asking the universe for something; you will certainly get what you ask for, but not always in the way you expect. Rather than a gift wrapped, front door delivery of what you hope for, you are sometimes provided with ways to help you work for what you're seeking. This gift of practice enables you to understand, cultivate, and receive. Hence the old adage, "Be careful what you wish for."

Despite the fact that I've learned multiple times to be aware of what I ask for, I thought with the ashram I deserved a weekend of peace, quiet, and sacrosanct introspection.

We make plans, my friends, and the universe sometimes giggles as it sets out an adventure of learning that circumvents our plans. So instead of finding peace during my weekend, I found the monster of turbulence, disruption and a fury of self-imposed negative stimulation in order to test out what I was seeking; the ability to find peace in all things, at all times.

This is what happened: I experienced a revelation about my obstacles to peace. I figured out, amidst the chaos and noise, that one of my biggest obstacles to peace was judgement. Judgment and criticism. I found myself repeatedly passing silent judgment and holding negative thoughts about aspects of the experience. The food, other guests, and teachings of the ashram were all fodder for my mental judgment and criticism gauntlet.

My awareness didn't dawn in an ethereal mountaintop meditation. It didn't come in a zen epiphany or a sudden realization. Rather, it was a gradual unfolding, a dawning awareness of the thoughts, conversations and stories which were continually presenting themselves during mediation, asana practice and lectures. In the moments I was hoping to find peace, I found an inner critic who just wanted to complain, bitch, and moan.

Once the pattern revealed itself, the message was clear: *I* am my biggest obstacle to peace. My sacred path to peace is paved with my own considerations.

"Judge nothing, you will be happy. Forgive everything, you will be happier. Love everything, you will be happiest." - **Sri Chinmoy**

What is your purpose? If I asked you this question today, what would you say? Life purpose, not job purpose. Why are you on this earth?

I'll tell you what I think. I think we have a common purpose, one universal to the entirety of the human race. I believe our deepest purpose is to connect to our highest self and to other living beings. The Harvard University Grant Study spanned seventy five years and examined a myriad of factors which contributed to people's sense of living a purposeful life. Researchers concluded that the most important determinant of happiness, for the majority of people, is human connection.

So how do we authentically connect to our highest self and to other living beings?

The path to true connection is narrow, and few will find it. Authentic connection, and ensuing happiness, can be achieved through love and a surrender of judgment.

OK, done. You can stop reading this book because I've just provided the answer to all questions you had about life, death and the world. Boom! One and done, baby. You are a rockstar.

Still here? Ah, yes, the acts of loving people and surrendering judgment can be more difficult than they initially seem. Love, we tend to feel okay about, but judgement, not so much. Most of us, if we take an honest look within, will find that we have room for improvement in the judgment department.

If you assess yourself honestly, how often are the following symptoms present?

» You rate others based on how they dress, the color of skin, where they live, their political choices, or how they parent.

» You become more enraged about others 'sins' than you are embarrassed by your own.

» You leave little to no room for mistakes made by others.

» You refuse to forgive; if you forgive, you refuse to forget.

» You cut off those that disagree with you, or you only listen to respond.

» You gossip and look forward to hearing gossip.

» You write off someone as hopeless (or worse).

Do any (or all) of these apply to you? In full honesty, they did, and sometimes still do, apply to me. During my ashram weekend I came into full acknowledgment that I was failing myself and others because I was constantly judging.

Some of this knowledge came full force from karmic revolutions in my own world. I was reaping what I'd sown and it was very, very painful.

Why should you stop judging or criticizing? If you want to experience joy and fulfillment- and, what I was seeking the most- peace, you have to put the brakes on judging. No one who judges others will truly experience happiness. No one who judges others will live up to their fullest potential. None. I don't know one happy, joyful, peaceful person who sits in criticism or judgment of others. Do you?

Remember when I said the universe provides ways to practice that which you desire the most? This is how we build our strength and ability to fully expand and reach our potential. Let's get real: not every day is one of spiritual expansion and reaching our potential. Somedays, sometimes, I want to stay right here at the bottom, with a ~~glass~~ bottle of wine and pretend I don't know any better while I gossip, criticize, and judge.

Why? Because internal growth can be painful, difficult and frustrating. Are you re-thinking this whole 'becoming a better person' thing now? I feel you. Strengthening our muscles is work. Have you ever looked at a body builder and thought, "Easy peasy, no problem, I can look like that, too"? If so, let me help wake you up: that shit is hard work. It takes a discipline, practice, and a deep sense of passion to commit and attain excellence. The same principles apply to surrendering judgement (and most of the chapters in this book). Learning to easily flex our happiness muscles requires doing some spiritual weight lifting.

After my weekend at the ashram, I returned to the real world, committed to release my patterns of judgment and criticism. Excited about exploring what my world would look like without this lens of ugliness, I felt connected to all beings through peace and love. I was all in, watching rays of sunshine coming out of everyone's asses through my rose colored glasses.

I was on the connection train to peace town, committed to experiencing life differently.

The first test of my newfound equanimity took place just days after I departed the ashram. I scheduled a day of self-care and goal-setting in Orange County California with my cousin and my podcast partner. My morning consisted of spin class and brunch with my cousin, the afternoon held plans for recording podcast episodes with my podcast partner and friend, and the evening promised a lovely dinner at a high rated plant based restaurant. Some of my very favorite things to do and people to see. Should be easy as hell to practice my non-judgement lenses.

Suffice it to say, things didn't go as planned. My judgment muscle was tested and I didn't exactly pass with flying colors. Shortly after arriving to the studio, ready to sweat and die, I walked into the spin room. There I saw the spin instructor and my inner judge brought the mental gavel down with a quickness.

"*She* is teaching this class?" My inner critic sneered at the teacher. "She doesn't look like she has spun, like, ever."

Yes, that was my first, shiny new rose-colored lens of non-judgment thought. What. The. F*&K. *Ugly*. The weight of my judgment failure hit me like a ton of bricks. Realizing my inadequacy, I spent most of the class crying like a blubbering idiot. Thank goodness it was dark and loud because otherwise it would have just been messy and embarrassing.

Ready for another universal truth bomb? Judgment and ugliness is almost always a reflection of ourselves.

My snap judgment of the spin instructor was, without a doubt, a reflection of myself. Upon carefully examining my ugly thoughts about her, I found that they were rooted tightly in a little nugget of my own fear and insecurities.

I host and teach yoga and thought transformation retreats around the country. I don't always teach the yoga part any more, as my specific passion is on thought transformation workshops. Nevertheless, in the past, and sometimes still, I teach yoga. However, I think I kinda suck at it. I can't memorize the flowing sequences, and I always forget Sanskrit names for the postures. Despite having been a student of yoga for over twenty years, I am still not able to get into many advanced postures, thus can't really effectively teach them. Icing on the cake? I unfailingly jack up everyone's left and rights. All this struggle exists despite taking not just one teacher training course, but *two* 200 hour certification courses.

As I judged this woman's ability to teach an effective spin class by her looks alone, I brought to light my own insecurity and perceived judgment in teaching yoga classes. I felt that students found me incompetent and wanting. I spent that entire spin class riding the hills and valleys of my emotions. First, I felt mad at myself for failing so miserably at my efforts of non-judgment, but as I spun my little heart out, sobbing ridiculously, the anger slowly, very slowly turned to this tiny bubble of hope and joy. I rejoiced for caring so deeply, for noticing and learning, because the old Shannon would have just thought the ugly thought, got on the bike and spun without the balm of healing that occurred through my tears and awareness. In mourning my judgmental self, I took a step towards healing myself and my own insecurity.

Pedaling, sweating, and crying, I realized that there was no difference between us. I am her, she is me, and we are one. Tears then fell in gratitude for the profound sense of connection. Instead of projecting my own fears and negativity onto another person, I realized through that spin class that I have the ability to send love and gratitude and simultaneously receive the same in any situation in which I would have normally had a knee jerk judgment reaction.

We absolutely, one hundred percent, receive back what we put out. We get what we give and reap what we sow. If you want to be accepted, accept others. If you want to feel loved, love others. If you want to feel peace, act peaceful to others. If you want to feel elevated, lift others up. If you want to feel abundant, give freely to others.

By the way, that was seriously the best damn spin class I have ever taken, hands down. I travel a lot, domestically and internationally, and have been to over thirty different spin studios worldwide. The instructor whom I was so quick to judge kicked ass, every ass in the room in fact, including my own. Rock on, sister.

Every single person we come in contact with has something special to offer to us, a gift, if we are open to receive it. Yes, even the assholes. It may be a gift of knowledge, higher awareness, or the gift of exercising our patience muscle. The very best gift others give us is the gift of self awareness, wrapped up in the opportunity to examine our reactions.

How you react to others says more about you than it does about them. Judging others is a tactic of the ego to avoid facing something uncomfortable about ourselves. By exploring beliefs and assumptions, instead of judging or criticizing, you are allowing yourself to expand to a higher self awareness, but more importantly, a higher self acceptance.

Ultimately when we judge or criticize, it is only a reflection; we project our own fears, insecurities and feelings of inadequacy onto others. By exploring rather than judging, we heal ourselves, remove blocks and limitations and find a sense of peace and joy within ourselves.

Steps for releasing judgment:

> » **Awareness or mindfulness.** Congratulations! You've already started this step. Just reading this chapter has made you more aware of how and why we judge. The next step is to recognize it when it happens, as it happens; and as it does, be kind to yourself. Maybe you don't spend 45 minutes on a spin bike crying about it, but do give yourself a break- this is a practice. Practice makes progress, and patient practice makes permanent.

» **Approach it in gratitude.** Gratitude is a game changer. When you start to judge or criticize, instead say to yourself, "Thank you for this opportunity for self awareness and self acceptance."

» **Actively look for the good in the people and situations you find yourself judging or criticizing.** Find something positive to focus on and let it be genuine. It doesn't have to be major, but could be as simple as, "What a beautiful scarf she is wearing."

» **Reframe it.** One way I help shape my judgmental thoughts is to reframe them. This works with regard to both others and ourselves. For instance, the thought, "She is so disorganized and messy" is a reflection of our own feelings or fears of being disorganized or inadequate. Reframe the thought as: "Wow! That girl is so creative and not confined by rigid structures." Instead of thinking, "He has no talent," which is a reflection of our own fear, jealousy, and insecurity, try: "He strives to do the best he can, as do I, and I celebrate us".

» **Lean on your tribe.** There is nothing more encouraging than a positive tribe you can trust to help when you are lost in a world of judgement, self condemnation and fear. This is such an important tool in your shed of happiness. Surround yourself with others who consciously seek to reframe their own judgement and criticism.

My prayer/ask of the universe:

Thank you for allowing me to release judgment of myself and others. Thank you for allowing me to send out love and open up to receive love through my acceptance and connection to everyone. Thank you for embracing that we are all connected, and that we are all one.

Questions to ponder:

Think of your most recent judgment- how is it linked to your own fears/insecurities?

_____

_____

_____

What is your own personal mantra in order to feel more connected?

_____

_____

_____

> *Judging others is actually a judgment of ourselves. It's useless and hurtful-kinda like drinking wine from a broken glass.* - **Shannon Jamail**

Comparison

Whatever your passion is, keep doing it. Don't waste time chasing after success or comparing yourself to others. Every flower blooms at a different pace. - **Suzy Kassem**

Growing up, I was often told by well-meaning adults that I was pretty, charming, or smart. On the surface, this seems like a positive thing, right? Showering children with accolades can only serve to boost their self-esteem, we often think. But, when we provide praise in this way, we're often unknowingly labeling our kids as well.

For me, attachment to these labels and affirmation of them became a craving, an addiction to reinforcement of my identity as a "pretty, charming, smart" girl. The labels others ascribed to me became the characteristics through which I built my value and worth. As I began paying attention to the ways others perceived me, I also gained awareness of how I stacked up in comparison to other girls. The same person who called me pretty described another girl as beautiful. I heard a teacher say I was smart, but my classmate was a genius. These subtle comparisons planted seeds in my heart which grew into feelings of inadequacy. I listened intently when people talked about me to hear how they viewed me in relation to others.

Constant comparison and subsequent silent competition prickled my skin and tainted my heart. It left me feeling unsettled and a little nauseous, all the time, as I walked on eggshells, wondering if the world would judge me to be good enough. I found myself constantly battling, navigating an ongoing invisible war between myself and others, and between myself and my better self - the one I knew I could be, if I just worked a little harder. I scrutinized other young ladies, studied their behaviors, grooming, and nuances, in an effort to figure out just how I might gain better titles, better labels. My energy was consumed with

31

figuring out answers to "How is *she* prettier, smarter, or more charming than I am?"

I was desperate to be needed, liked, included, and valued. Most of all, I was desperate to be seen and labeled as either good enough or better than my peers. I constantly found myself jumping right to comparison in my own conversations, or intruding upon conversations of others, yearning to insert myself and my importance into their lives.

Envy drove me to perpetuate the cycle of comparison between myself and others whenever possible. Conversations in comparison and competition often went like this:

> Person: "I recently visited Yellowstone. It was so awesome and I stayed at this great hotel..."

> Me: "Oh yes, I've been there! That hotel was lovely, though I stayed at this other one that was a bit more luxurious."

In needing to be better than other people, I became a one-upping interrupter. I'd even go so far as to say things which were untrue, with the hopes of impressing my listeners.

> Person: "I heard there are gonna be some big changes around the office and that So-and-so is going to get promoted..."

> Me: "Oh, really? That's interesting. I know all about the changes, but I heard that So-and-so's numbers are not as good as my team's numbers so that is interesting that he might be promoted."

Upon hearing news that was favorable for someone else, instead of celebrating them, I immediately jumped to comparison, competition, and justification of myself and my worth.

> Person: "I have over 10k followers on Instagram now, I am so excited! I can't believe it!"

Me: "Good for you. I actually don't spend that much time on social media so that I can truly invest in what is important in life. But everyone's different."

When confronting circumstances which trigger feelings of not being enough, I deflected them by indirectly tearing someone else down. It can be hard to remember that other people's successes are not our failures.

Person: "Ooooh I love that woman's dress! It looks gorgeous on her!"

Me: "It is a pretty dress! Not sure I would have picked it for her frame though. It's not exactly the most flattering."

When hearing someone else receive a compliment, rather than simply be happy for them, a need for validation and a compliment of my own drove me to insult someone else.

I could write out hundreds of conversations like the ones above, some which took place out loud, and countless more which only occurred in my head. Internal conversations like this are equally destructive as those which take place out loud - they still reinforce the cycle of comparison and competition. They still create negative energy within, which will inevitably be sent out into the world. Whether it seems harmless or not, and regardless of whether another person is involved in the comparison game, the end result is always the same: feelings of unworthiness and the belief that there is not enough for all of us.

This constantly comparing jerk was me. Sometimes, on bad days, it still is. Comparison, the close cousin of judgement, happens to most of us on a daily - hourly - momently basis - and it requires vigilance to alter the cycle! When we compare ourselves to others, we not only disregard and disrespect our own unique value, but we miss out on the joy of celebrating others and realizing that there is enough awesomeness in life for everyone.

"Comparison is the thief of joy." - **Theodore Roosevelt**

Comparison is a roadblock to love. It steals our ability to feel contentment and fulfillment, spiraling us into self doubt, causing us to question everything we do, who we are, and what is our value in the world. The cycle of comparison and competition inevitably leads to the same place: the low, lonely pit of believing we are not enough.

How you know you are stuck in the comparison game:

» It is difficult for you to celebrate the success of those around you - their success feels like your failure.

» You find yourself criticizing friends and family while scrolling through social media.

» When something good happens to anyone else, you wonder why it didn't happen to you.

» You find yourself justifying your career, means, or status when looking at someone else's.

» You feel you are not where you want to be at this stage of your life, not because of your own specific goals, but because of where peers are in their lives.

» You get angry, frustrated or jealous (or experience a feeling of 'less than') when something amazing falls into the lap of someone you call a friend or family member.

Comparison robs us of opportunities for growth and expansion. When we encounter another person's success, we have two main options: We can compare ourselves to them, find ourselves wanting, and tear them down, perpetuating the cycle of unworthiness. Or, we can alter the course by choosing instead to celebrate and initiate.

Compare and tear down? Or celebrate and initiate? I, for one, love a good party, so I'll opt for the celebration instead. When we honor another person's success by congratulating them, celebrating them, and recognizing the effort they have committed to achieve their success, we pour love out into the world, lift each other up, and perpetuate a cycle of encouragement.

After celebrating, initiate! Take the opportunity to initiate a new stage of growth and expansion in your life by asking: What can I learn from this person's success? How can I connect with them to cultivate more of this in my own life? Honor their achievement by inquiring, "I love how you did this, do you have any advice you can share?"

Sometimes we are viewing other people's success from afar, and it's difficult to find the authentic connection which allows us to genuinely celebrate them. There are many forums where it is easier to compare, like social media. Social media, with it's carefully curated captions, and filtered glossy images, makes it easy for us to compare our behind-the-scenes with everyone else's highlight reel.

It's important to remember that every single person - let me say that again, *every single person,* who is posting on social media is a human being, just like you. They have heartache and struggle, just like you. They experience grief and loss, just like you. They know pain and will die, just like you. And just like you are feeling comparison by looking at someone else, *someone else is feeling comparison when looking at you.*

Social media is a strange animal. Despite being more digitally connected than ever, most of the people I talk to - family, clients, friends - all report feeling isolation, loneliness, and unworthiness in direct correlation with the amount of time they spend consuming social media. What does this mean? It means that all the liking, thumbs-upping, hearting, tweeting, re-gramming, blogging, vlogging, or sharing in the world isn't going to fill our deep, universal, human need for real connection with others.

Here's a personal story of my own experience with the deceptiveness of social media. A really close friend of mine used to frequently post amazing pictures of her and her husband. In their photos, they always looked beautiful, put-together, stylish, and happy. This friend of mine posted often - at least twice a week - elaborate posts about how much she loved her husband, how wonderful he was, and how awesome their life was together. I found myself annoyed at the extent of their digital PDA, to the point where I said to myself, "Good grief, give it a rest already. Get a room!"

Here is what I didn't know: my friend was buried in pain and suffering, and the photos and posts were her way of trying to save face. They were her way of trying to fake it til they made it - only, they didn't make it. One afternoon she texted me: "The husband and I split up. I don't want to talk about it, but just in case you hear about it another way, I wanted you to know." I was shocked. What the heck? How is that possible? Yesterday, she was posting dreamy, lovey dovey photos, and today, they are kaput? This is an example of the highlight reel, alternatively called the "my life is falling apart but I am determined to put masking tape and silly string on it for the world to see" reel.

If social media serves you, that's awesome, use it. If it supports your business, super, take advantage of it. If it helps you reach family and friends who live far away, brilliant, connect with it! Just remember that behind every picture, video, and post, is a living, breathing, bleeding human seeking the surge of dopamine that comes when someone else, through a fleeting moment of digital connection, affirms or validates their worth.

Ways you can free yourself from comparison:

> » **Immediately celebrate.** Fake it if you have to. When you see someone else's accomplishments, especially those you might

compare yourself to or tear down, instead, say "I celebrate you!" Don't worry about feeling or looking goofy. Say it. Eventually you will feel it, and so will the universe, which will in turn send it back to you.

» **There is enough for everyone.** My friend and podcast partner Dee helped me see this so clearly. The universe is *vast and abundant.* There is enough money for everyone. There is enough business for everyone. There is enough travel for everyone. It is our job to seek it, but there is enough. Feeling anything else is coming from a place of lack- which in turn will provide more lack.

» **Go into creation mode.** Time spent consuming and comparing is time wasted. Move from consumption mode into creation mode. Get off of social media. Get away from things that stir up those feelings of inadequacy and dig into what you are passionate about. Your life is a canvas to your imagination. I dare you to believe that anywhere you find comparison, you can also find creation and the opportunity to cultivate that goodness in your own life.

» **Make a self-love list.** Create a list of amazing things others have said about you. I have an email folder in which I put all accolades I get from clients, friends and family members. I have a box of cards and notes that have been mailed to me over the years that celebrate me too. When I am feeling particularly down and susceptible to comparison, and my other tools are not working- I go through these reminders.

» **Find your grateful heart.** While we are scouring the world for what everyone has or is doing, we forget the beautiful things that surround us. And those things get neglected, dusty and unused. Then they disappear altogether. Stop and take inventory of the many things that are perfectly shiny and amazing all around you. Right now.

My prayer/ask of the universe:

Thank you for allowing me to see with my heart and not with the desperation of my ego. Thank you for celebrating others, for allowing me to lift them up in praise and for knowing that I am enough. I am enough. I am enough.

Questions to ponder:

When was the last time you compared yourself to others:

_____

_____

_____

Where were you and what can you do differently?

_____

_____

_____

PART 2

Trust

Pain

> *Pain is temporary. It may last a minute, or an hour, or a day, or a year, but eventually it will subside and something else will take its place. If I quit, however, it lasts forever.* - **Lance Armstrong**

At the beginning of 2017, I was living a hot streak. I mean, I was smoking hot, fireworks, winning at life. My world was on fire in a good way. Business, relationships and even my parenting efforts felt incredible. Spiritually, I was empowered: my energy felt cosmic and I was attuned and aligned with my belief system. I felt full of faith, inspiration, and connection to the divine. Bouts with anxiety were infrequent, almost non-existent in fact, and my ability to handle family or business crises was solid. In short, I was burning and brimming with passion, excitement, motivation, and confidence. Nothing could bring me down... or so I thought.

With one phone call, my forward momentum came to a screeching halt and the fire of my success was doused with a big old bucket of icy cold reality. My world tilted on its axis when I received word that one of my children was on the way to the hospital with a grave, possibly life threatening situation. In the span of one short conversation, I went from rocking and rolling at life to reeling in shock at the situation unfolding before me. In just a few moments, with just a few words, I was brought to my knees, crippled by the gut-wrenching pain of knowing my child was suffering.

Evaluating pain can easily become a comparison game as we stack our difficulties against the suffering of others. Whether weighing our own anguish, or considering the pain of others, there's a common pitfall of trying to measure pain in an attempt to rationalize or justify the devastation it creates in our lives.

Such attempts to measure pain are often well-intentioned efforts to remind people that things could be worse. We've all heard the well meaning friend say, "Oh you think that is bad, well last year...," or "My situation may not be as bad or difficult as yours, but..." and continue on to stack your pain against their own. These misguided attempts to mitigate pain fail spectacularly every time, because.... there is no greater pain than what one is feeling at that moment. The truth is, there can be no comparison amongst our subjective realities. Comparison itself is a falsehood: There is no level playing field with the human experience. Whatever pain one is going through is unequivocally the worst kind of pain, in that moment, for them, and it can't be compared or contrasted with another's pain.

When I heard the news that my child was going into the hospital, situation tenuous, prognosis unknown, I was riddled with fear, uncertainty, and self blame. It was, without a doubt, the worst kind of pain.

In retrospect, if I hadn't been rooted firmly in a place of security, strength, and confidence, the news would have shattered me completely. If I hadn't been vibrating at my highest level, receiving word of my child's suffering could have easily landed me in the next hospital bed, overwhelmed by grief, anxiety, and depression. Thankfully, my reserve of strength and faith lent itself to making me one pissed off mama bear instead of a weepy, inconsolable, ineffective mess. Rather than allow the pain to paralyze me, I channeled it into anger. I responded by raging at the universe, "Are you kidding me?!" I was heartbroken for my child, but also for myself. I found myself asking God and the universe the questions that we so often ask when encountering pain: "Why is this happening? Why to my child?"

Why wasn't the right question. It never is, for pain. Once time passes, we can often see that the purpose behind pain is to draw us closer to the divine, and to ourselves as pain forces us to dig deeper into our source of strength, faith, and hope. But in the apex of pain, asking "why" is futile.

The question that needed to be asked instead is "How? How do I show up in love and be what is needed right now? How do I embrace this pain?"

I believe now, it is only because I'd been "on fire" that I was able to walk through this pain without being burned, without my world completely crumbling around me. If I had not been equipped by the internal work I'd done up to that point, I feel quite sure that the subsequent turmoil, the emotional and mental suffering that followed would have spun me out of control. If I hadn't been practicing how to sit with pain, I would have been toast. At least, for a while, I'd have been paralyzed, immobile and unable to show up and be a mom to my other kids, a wife to my husband, a businesswoman and, most importantly, my own supportive ally.

What does it mean to practice sitting with pain? Pain isn't something that we usually invite into our lives. Humans, as a species, generally try to avoid it. We have biological predispositions to avoid it, protective warning systems hardwired into our neurology which are designed for self-preservation. Whether it is an open emotional wound from childhood, a broken relationship, or physical pain of any sort, whatever the kind of pain - we tend to avoid it, numb it or run from it.

The hard truth is this: pain is a necessary part of the human experience. Emotions that lead to pain (shame, guilt, anxiety, anger) are vital pathways to personal and spiritual growth. These challenging emotions have the ability to bring us closer to our true selves and reason for existence - to live and connect in love. These unpleasant but powerful growth tools also help us to understand and connect with the world around us. Without pain, humans would have no empathy, no compassion. Without pain, there would be no growth and transformation. Without pain, we would have no access to higher conscious learning. Pain is one of life's greatest teachers. It is often a necessary Trojan horse, conquering our defenses and breaching our walls to invade, destroy what is no longer serving us. Only through this destruction can we rebuild, stronger and wiser than we were before.

Sometimes pain comes in small doses, little moments that we think are no big deal, and we shuffle them away, hiding them inside ourselves. They build up slowly, layers of dust, until we find ourselves suffocating in a dirt fortress built of our own making.

Last year I worked with a client who was continuously let down by her parents. She felt as if her support system comprised of her in-laws and a couple other family members, but anytime she needed her parents help, even if just for an encouraging word, she would be blown off, rebuffed and even sometimes degraded. In one particular situation she was in a bind with her children and really needed help due to a scheduling conflict. In her mind, her parents lived minutes away, and were retired- should be no big deal to just pick up her kids from location A and take to location B. I mean she didn't need them to babysit, she just needed them picked up from one location and taken to another that was only minutes apart. Should take her parents a total of 30 minutes from start to finish. Easy right? Not really. They were unable to assist with no real explanation or reason. Her in law drove over two hours to pick up her children from a location and drop to another location that were minutes apart from each other, though her in law had to spend four hours on the road. She came to me in pain. "What is wrong with me? There must be something wrong with me that they just are not there for us. Maybe I am unlovable."

"Why does there have to be something wrong with you? Why can't it be about them?"

She had never been asked this before. We spent time reframing the situations and taking a deeper look into her pain.

During this, she considered how unfair her thinking was. Perhaps her parents were afraid to step up to the task of caring for her children (even just in driving them). Perhaps her parents are worried about doing something wrong, or things not going as planned, or was simply overwhelmed with the thought of helping. Yes, perhaps they just didn't want to, but wasn't that ok too? Weren't they allowed to feel any way they wanted to? Upon her sorting through her own reactions, alternative perspectives and her own heart-she realized that ultimately, their choice had nothing to do with her or her kids. Just like that, the dirt was gone.

With this sifting process, she felt a release of tension and frustration and found herself resting in a place of love. During a particular session we did a meditation in which I called to her mind's eye her parents, and asked her to inwardly speak to them, voicing the resolution her heart needed: "It is ok, I love you and I am loved." Instantaneously, she experienced a profound sense of peace and comfort. She learned two lessons through this situation. One: A painful event, regardless of size or intensity, is always an opportunity for growth, expansion and a key to self awareness. Two: Pain is never really about who we think it is. Blaming, shaming, and accusing have no place in navigating the hardship of pain. It's a lesson and opportunity to explore the question: What am I missing, feeling, experiencing through this hurt?

> *Your pain is the breaking of the shell that encloses understanding.*
> **- Khalil Gibran**

Pain is also a catalyst for transformation, a natural steroid shot of strength. Pain allows us to sift what is no longer needed and identify our weaknesses. If we let it, pain can reveal how our lowest points of weakness can be transformed into our highest badass points of strength. The truth is, if there were no pain, we couldn't fully appreciate the beauty either. As Glennon Doyle, best-selling author and activist likes to point out, the world is brutiful (both brutal and beautiful.) We wouldn't see, appreciate, or understand the beauty without the brutal parts.

The trouble for many of us is that we get stuck in our pain. We may feel temporary relief of our pain, and then someone or something occurs that reopens a wound. Or, after a significantly painful event, perhaps the wound never closes or heals, if we don't find closure or consciously work through the lesson. Ongoing unidentified emotional pain can cause anxiety, depression, digestion issues, and somatic or physical pain.

Some signs you may be stuck in pain:

» You get defensive easily - carrying pain that has not been embraced causes bitterness and defensiveness in all areas of our lives.

» When you think of certain situations, you immediately get mad or sad.

» When you see or think of someone that has caused you pain, you start to imagine how you could hurt them back and hope or wish to see karma work in your favor.

» When certain memories come to mind you feel lost or as if you are drowning.

There is rebirth in pain and suffering. In Buddhist doctrine, it is believed that only through suffering can full enlightenment occur. And although I don't seek pain, or recommend one to do so, I no longer run from it either. Rather I embrace the pain, acknowledge it's lessons and remind myself that growth, compassion and a higher self awareness is occurring. It also comforts me to remember that pain leads me to become stronger in ways that will help me, my children or someone else in the future.

Pain ought not to be measured or compared.

One of my newest clients recently asked me, "How long is the right amount of time to grieve?" She lost both of her parents three years earlier, back to back deaths, and found herself stuck in a cycle of immobility and dysfunction. Her physical health deteriorated and she frequently experienced feeling unwell and ill. Her constant sickness left her unable to work.

There is no one-size-fits-all timeline for healing from grief. Despite what some mental health practitioners or experts say, there isn't a schedule for it. I have heard some people say that pain or grief can last forever. I don't accept that either. I believe we are changed forever, but we should not be in pain forever. One of the reasons we get stuck - whether it is a day, three years, or a lifetime - is because we haven't allowed the growth and transformation to occur. We have been busy blocking it, numbing it, running from it. Sadly, these behaviors not only extend the timeline of grief, but compound the pain as well, so that each time it surfaces, it can be even more debilitating.

The key to transforming pain into power is to embrace it.

Steps to embracing pain:

» **Thank the pain.** Thank the pain for the transformation that is occurring with a trust that it is happening as it should without expectation, timelines or resistance.

» **Ask: what can I learn from this?** Seek the lesson, as if you were on the outside looking in. What would you say or tell someone else about this situation?

» **Forgiveness.** Consider offering forgiveness to other people involved, not necessarily for them, but for yourself. Holding on to pain, caused by someone else, is like you drinking poison and hoping the other person will die. Do this at your pace, with grace and compassion.

» **Embrace with knowledge.** Understand that the more we embrace pain, the more we allow transformation to occur, the more we can evolve into a higher consciousness.

» **Grace. Grace. Grace.** Offer yourself grace and love through the process.

My prayer/ask of the universe:

Thank you for the transformation and opportunity to grow during this time. Thank you for the support and for holding me up in grace and love. Thank you for the strength needed during this time. Please open my heart and allow forgiveness to enter. Please allow me to embrace this experience and to view what is happening in love.

Questions to ponder:

What was the last painful experience you had?

_____

_____

_____

How can you view and surrender that experience in love?

_____

_____

_____

Silence

"Silence is a source of great strength." - **Lao Tzu**

During one of my internships for my masters degree, I worked at a clinic where my primary client base consisted of people who were court ordered to attend therapy. Often, they were diagnosed with co-occuring disorders, which means suffering from addiction as well as another mental health disorder. This particular group of clients is one of the toughest demographics for mental health practitioners to work with, because the clients don't want to change and generally have no desire to be there. It is one thing when a client walks into my office with the desire — not the discipline or ability or even capacity — just a *desire* to change. It is another thing entirely when they are court ordered to be there; the phrase "uphill battle" comes to mind.

Working with clients who aren't ready to work means I have spent many sessions in silence. I've passed hour after hour staring eye to eye with my clients, without any verbal exchange at all.

I recall one of the first times I sat with a court ordered client, who came in like a brick wall, closed off, shut down, and not just quiet, but *silent*. After cursory introductions, we sat looking at each other, waiting for the work to begin. Nothing happened. My inquiry for them to share a little about themselves was firmly rebuffed by a blanketing wall of silence. Confident that a patient and willing demeanor would entice my client to speak, I settled back in my chair and waited for them to open up, get vulnerable, and get to work on creating meaningful change. I sat, and I waited, and the silence stretched out between us. Staring at each other became awkward, and then painful. I shifted in my seat, cleared my throat, glanced at the clock, and tapped my pencil on my notepad.

Saying this was uncomfortable is putting it mildly. I felt as if I needed to speak, to fill the silence or gap, to do *something*, because the silence made me want to poke my own eyes out. Checking the clock, I realized the desire to poke out my eyes occurred within the first sixty seconds of a fifty minute session.

After the first or second time this happened, I went to my clinical supervisor completely exasperated. I was certain that she'd steer me in the right direction to help get my clients talking. After all, that's what I was there for — I was their *therapist*, for crying out loud!

"This is feeling ridiculous," I said, "how am I supposed to help initiate change when the client just sits in silence?"

My supervisor smiled comfortably at me and said nothing in reply.

I stared at her. She stared at me. Silence.

Thirty seconds turned to a minute, and still, crickets.

The silence stretched out between us, long enough that my eye-poking impulse started to rear it's ugly head, and still my supervisor did not speak. Slowly, almost painstakingly slowly, the realization dawned on me: Silence is golden. In silence, we do the deep work. Silence provides the space to *be:* not to live up to, not to placate, not to fulfill, but to just *be*.

I left her office encouraged and fortified, ready to simply sit and let the magic happen. My new mental mantra resounded quietly within me: *Silence is the place to be.* I carried this mantra with me and let it affirm me through many silent hours. After several months of working with my silent clients, I started to see small but miraculous changes happening. First, quiet, cleansing tears. Then whispers of acceptance, followed by encompassing compassion.

Even more miraculous than the changes in my clients, were the changes occurring in *me*. As I sat in silence, vibrating with love and compassion for my client, I felt the same vibration eventually echo back to me, and in the peace of the silence, I received it. As I sat in quiet reflection, focused on peace and healing for my client, I felt the same take place in me.

It's common in western culture today to talk a lot but say very little. We often use words to satisfy someone else, distract from discomfort, or appease a socially awkward situation. We mindlessly chatter to fill the gap, the silent space in which we feel most vulnerable — but also most connected.

Sitting with silence allows us to not only tune out distractions, but to tune in to each other and really listen. Silence allows us to focus on our internal landscape without thinking about what we will say, how we'll respond, or what's coming next. Resting in silence enables us to look closer, observe more keenly, to pay ourselves — and others — the attention we so deeply need.

Silence also teaches us the courage to transcend avoidance. All too often, we sit around, faces in our phones, trying to block out the 'noise' of living. It is easy to drown out thoughts or feelings with television, social media, drugs and alcohol, but silence teaches us courage — the courage to face *ourselves*.

Silence leads us to recognize truth. Lies buried within become glaringly apparent when there is nothing but quiet and the space to examine them.

Silence helps us remember that simplicity is peace: the rise and fall of the chest with each breath, the steady drum of our heartbeats. We begin to hear life's symphony: birds calling to each other, leaves blowing in the breeze, the sounds of humanity around us.

Silence guides us into receptive connection. We are accustomed to surface connection, filled with small talk and business cards. Silence offers the deeper energetic connection of being in a space with loved ones, or even strangers, and simply *being*.

Signs you may need silence:

» You feel a tightness in your chest when you think about the day ahead of you.

» When stressful thoughts come up, you immediately consider having a drink, a drug, a cigarette, or watching tv.

» You are feeling overwhelmed, overworked, or under-appreciated.

» You have a knee-jerk reaction to those who hurt you, and respond in unkind or rude ways.

» During any and every free moment you have, you immediately get on your phone and scroll through social media, texts or reply to email.

Somehow, in silence, the areas that need healing, heal themselves.

We are all driven by desire. Desire can manifest in a healthy way as goals or ambition, but it can also present itself as cravings or undefined wants - the feeling that there is something outside of us that we need in order to be complete, whole, or happy. We aren't always conscious of this mild sense of dissatisfaction lurking beneath the surface, but it reveals itself in a myriad of ways: binge eating, mindless scrolling on social media, or ordering things we don't need online. We often respond to the wants impulsively, only to find ourselves feeling empty again a short time later.

Spending time in silence, in stillness, allows us to detach from these incessant wants, to observe them from a distance and analyze where they are coming from and why they arise. Just as food cravings often reveal a nutritional deficiency, life cravings often reveal a lack in an aspect of emotional or mental well-being, like self-care, self-confidence, or self-appreciation.

In silence, our deepest truths have space to bubble to the surface. Sitting in silence, we often hear the voice of our highest self — the one which gently guides us towards the person we want to become.

In high school, I made some horrible, terrible, no good, very bad choices. Aside from dropping out of high school my sophomore year, I also did not choose my friends wisely, and found myself socializing with people with questionable values and hanging out in shady, dangerous areas of ill repute. Most of my poor choices came from trying to be what I thought was the cool kid everyone would like.

During one of my trips into a real questionable 'hood', I was brought to a house that sold narcotics — like, the big time stuff. My friend left me in a room with one of the dealers who was only a few years older than myself, at the ripe old age of fourteen. My friend went into the other room to 'have some fun,' in the most dangerous ways possible. Seconds became minutes, minutes turned into hours as I sat, terrified, waiting for her to return.

At first I thought, I can do this. I can be cool and like, fit in. But my body wasn't getting the message of being cool, and instead of being relaxed and chill, I froze. My instinct was shouting, "GET THE F*&# OUT OF HERE," but my body literally would not move. The dealer tried to talk to me and convince me to 'have some fun,' but my paralysis and obvious terror won him over, and he finally gave up. I was literally like some frozen crazy white chick and I think I actually scared him a bit. He left me by myself in the room, in the dark, for hours. I never said a word. Never moved. I didn't blink, or close my eyes. Over and over, I repeated to myself silently, "I am ok. It will be ok. I am safe." It was the first time I meditated, though I had no idea that that's was what I was doing.

Eventually, my friend came back, and we left. I was furious at her, but of course, didn't say it. We parted ways, and as I walked to the city bus stop that night, I reflected a bit (as much as a lost teenager does), and realized that I didn't want to be the cool kid anymore. I didn't want to be the bad chick hanging out in some gangsters bedroom, wondering if I was going to be okay. I just wanted to be me.

Looking back now, that realization dawned on me in the interminable silence and solitude of that scary bedroom. If I had not sat there for hours, fear driven or not, I would not have awakened to the necessity of honoring myself, my convictions, and my truth. Had I not sat in terrified silence for hours on end, my life may have taken a very different path. In retrospect, those hours of silence probably saved my life.

Silence is also usually the best response when you find yourself wanting to spew hateful words, when it is hard, or impossible, to find a loving reply to the situation in which you find yourself. Has anyone told you, "If you don't have something nice to say, don't say anything at all?" Well, if not, consider yourself told.

When I was pregnant with my firstborn, I was a child myself, only eighteen years old. Now, I wasn't your average eighteen year old — I was already living on my own, working full time, going to college part time, and had already lived a couple of lifetimes by that point. My full time job was at a clothing retail store that I had been working at since I was just shy of sixteen. I rose through the ranks over the couple of years, and by the time I found out I was pregnant, I was assistant manager of the store, in line to manage my own store next. The unexpected pregnancy threw a teeny, tiny, baby-shaped wrench into my plans.

After I realized I was knocked up, my boss and mentor, someone whom I greatly admired and had learned a lot from, called me into the office to discuss my career trajectory with the company. He knew my situation; pregnant, not married, living on my own. Despite our usually easy rapport, there was a heaviness in the room, and he wouldn't quite look me in the eye. He fiddled with a stack of papers and cleared his throat a few times as I sat, waiting for him to tell me what the meeting was about. I could tell he was quite uncomfortable.

When he finally spoke, he simply said, "So, what is your plan?"

I had no idea what he was asking me. Had I missed something?

"My plan?" I parroted back, wondering if there was a new promotion or sale I was supposed to be organizing.

My mind started running. Why is he nervous? Did I mess up the deposit? I didn't steal anything..right?

He looked down at his hands and his voice dropped even lower. "You know, with the baby?"

Ahhh. Is this really happening? I sat, silent, wondering how he was going to fumble through this conversation.

"You know," he said evenly, "you are in line to get promoted, and having a baby can complicate things."

Are. You. Fucking. Kidding. Me? Was he really telling me that if I kept the baby (what in the hell gave him the idea that I wouldn't?) then I maybe wasn't going to get promoted?

I wanted to scream, cuss, and read him the riot act, but I didn't. I just sat there. I knew, beyond a shadow of a doubt, that I was a great employee. I may have been pregnant, full of shit, selfish and not quite right in the head at that point, but a bad employee I most certainly was *not*. I was a *stellar* employee.

Work ethic was in my blood — my parents, both of them, worked so hard their entire lives. My mother never completed high school, but instead of turning to welfare (which was the obvious easy answer), she worked multiple minimum wage jobs, busting her ass and setting an example for me that I've never forgotten. She worked nights, so she could care for my brother and me during the day, and she never called in sick, even when she was. My dad struggled with ongoing health problems but worked two jobs, always showing up at least an hour before he had to be there and doing twice as much as what was expected (at least). Their work effort and work ethic were badges of pride and honor, and they were also genetic. I didn't come from lazy stock. I was a kick ass worker.

As I sat with my boss, considering his question, a soapbox monologue about my hardworking genes ran through my head, but I didn't open my mouth to let him have it.

Instead, I sat in silence. As I did, another question arose in my mind: Would he be asking the plans of a *man* who found out his girlfriend or wife was pregnant?

The sexism and condescension, though well-intended, were glaringly obvious. My boss, mentor, and friend was failing to see that his attempt at help was backfiring, and creating a whole heap of hurt.

I sat in silence and stared at him, willing him to see the problem with what he was asking me. I couldn't respond because my heart was broken, and I didn't respond because I knew whatever was going to come out of my mouth wasn't going to be productive — not for my career, and not for my soul. I sat, psychically urging him to reconsider the conversation, as I zipped my lips and refused to utter even a single word.

I made the right choice. A few moments passed, and he realized the inappropriate nature of his question. Flustered, he backpedaled, and said something to the effect of, "I'm sure it will all work out. You're doing a great job. You're a smart young lady." I stood up, excused myself, and left the room.

Silence saved both of us — my boss, and myself — in that situation. For the record, I did get promoted, albeit later than originally intended, and along the way, my boss and mentor supported me a hundred percent. Through the journey of pregnancy, he saved me multiple times, as I was the sickest pregnant girl you ever met. After my promotion, he continued to mentor me for years, offering me guidance, compassion, and friendship as my gorgeous son came screaming into the world and

I tried to figure out how to balance motherhood, being a working mom, and growing up. For the record, I still haven't figured it out.

Silence is a gift, a blessing, and a necessity. Today, I seek silence regularly. My husband might call it hiding from the kids, but I call it resetting. I find it in my closet, on our boat dock, or in my car. Multiple times throughout the day, I take three to five minutes and just breathe. Each time I do, I find clarity — even if it's just clarity that today is a good day to be a good day. Sometimes it's clarity over a discussion with my husband, or how to communicate better with my kids. Other times, it's just the clarity to get over myself.

In silence, we can witness our issues. Recently, I attended my first yin yoga class. Whoa — talk about space for silence and deep work. If you're not familiar, yin is a form of yoga in which one holds postures for long periods of time - minutes on end, to allow stretching in connective tissue rather than muscles. I thought it was going to be relaxing... not exactly. It was deep work, physically and mentally. After about three minutes in a pose where my muscles were screaming to get out, the instructor said calmly, "Issues hide in our tissues." I sat, in silence, with my issues screaming in my tissues and the tears began to trickle out. I cried silently on my mat, and the process released physical and emotional tension that I didn't even know I was carrying. In that stillness and silence, I found the healing power of acceptance and just *being*.

Ways you can seek silence:

» Immerse yourself in nature. Head to the mountains, desert, or ocean. Or just go outside, take your shoes off and put your feet in the grass.

» Breathe. Do nothing else. 5 minutes.

» Small silence — just one minute. Put your phone, computer, and television away, and don't speak to anyone. Work up to 10 minutes. If 30 minutes is your jam — get there. If you find 10 minutes is your happy place- stay there.

» Go in your closet. Shut the door. Count your breaths.

» Check out a yin yoga class, silence retreat, or go for a long walk by yourself with no music, phones or distractions.

My prayer/ask of the universe:

Thank you for the very breath I take and the stillness within each inhale and exhale. Please allow me to find grace in silence and detach from any expectations.

Questions to ponder:

When a moment of stillness occurs — what is your immediate desire?

_____

_____

_____

_____

_____

List ways in which you can practice silence & stillness:

_____

_____

_____

———————————————————————————————

———————————————————————————————

———————————————————————————————

Among chaos and energetic vibrations, silence is a gift of internal work and immense peace. - **Shannon Jamail**

Tribe

When I was maybe ten or eleven I remember looking up to these two best friends, teenage girls who lived in my town. I wanted so badly to be like them. They were the "it" girls: pretty, popular and so much fun. My platonic crush on them went from admiration to emulation as I tried to make myself as cool as the girls. I loved everything about them, at least, I did before they were hired to babysit me and my younger brother.

The first time they watched us things went off without any problem. The girls let us play games, joked with us, and had us in bed mostly on time. As far as I know, while I was awake, they did exactly what they were supposed to do. But the second time, not so much.

On the second night the girls came to watch us, it was for an all night shift. My mother was working from 11pm to 7am, and the girls were staying at our apartment. My brother and I were in our pajamas waiting for the girls to arrive, excited at the prospect of hanging out with them. After my mom left, one of the girls put my brother to bed as the other one sat me down in the living room and spoke to me in a conspiring tone, like she was sharing a great secret with me, she said, "Ok, don't tell your mom but we invited our boyfriends over and we are gonna have a good time, okay? It's going to be so much fun." Her eyes sparkled and danced, and I nodded in a way that I hoped was nonchalant but probably looked like an eager Labrador puppy. I was over the moon, beyond excited that they thought of me as one of them and were going to let me hang out and have so much fun with them and their boyfriends! It was like someone had come and sprinkled magical fairy dust all over my evening.

As we waited for the boyfriends, I spun a vision in my mind of what we'd do: Throw pillows all over the floor, pop popcorn, drink soda, try on makeup, maybe even do something crazy, like play spin the bottle. Maybe we'd sneak outside and howl at the moon. We'd swap secrets, and I'd nonchalantly watch as the girls kissed their boyfriends good night. We'd become best friends that night. It would be so much fun.

No matter what the night held, I was ready to have a blast with the girls. My brother was in bed and one of the girls cracked open a couple of pops for us. We were laughing and watching TV, and I felt blanketed in the warm glow of the their acceptance.

Then everything seemed to go sideways. The boyfriends arrived and within a few short minutes the drugs came out and the girls and their boyfriends got loaded. Like, stoned out of their minds. The noise and excitement woke my little brother and he came out in the living room to see what was going on. Instead of sending him back to bed, one of the girls fixed her gaze on my younger brother, who was about eight or nine.

"Come here," she said.

Captivated by her, and too naive to know the difference, he came, and she proceeded to blow smoke from her joint directly into his face. He willingly inhaled, not knowing how the smoke would affect him. The boyfriends laughed hysterically, amused at how my brother scrunched his face up and closed his eyes as he inhaled. Emboldened and encouraged by their laughter, he decided this was a fun game, and so they kept playing until my brother was stoned out of his mind as well.

"You want some too?" asked one of the girls, her now glazed and reddened eyes looking me up and down, sizing me up to see if I was ballsy enough to go along with their party, or whether I was going to be a drag and bust them. I can still see clearly in my mind's eye the expression on the girls face that I looked up to. I can still feel the weight of her scrutiny, and the hopefulness bubbling in my chest that I would be cool enough, that I wouldn't say or do the wrong thing. Mustering up my best cool-girl mystique, I replied, "Sure. Yeah. I want some."

I wanted to fit in. I wanted to be liked. I wanted to feel accepted. I wanted to be her friend. But deep down, I didn't really want the pot. I didn't really want to do drugs. I didn't want to get in trouble, or lead my brother into danger, or do anything illegal. I found myself between a rock and a hard place. I wanted desperately for the girls to like me, to be cool like them, but in the back of my mind (or maybe deep in the pit of my belly) I felt a little voice telling me to be cautious. Thankfully, my lying skills were in full strength at the ripe old age of tenish. I pretended to inhale, which is not nearly as hard as it sounds when the person blowing at you can't hardly see your face. I let them blow smoke at me and even faked being stoned, though they weren't paying much attention because my brother was putting on quite the show to keep everyone entertained.

Looking back, I'm not sure what kept me from joining in that night. Despite my reservations, it wasn't like I was some saint in regards to taking drugs. I was willing to be bad to have friends, but something was holding me back. My best guess is that I had seen quite a bit of self destruction, violence and pain by then, mostly involving drugs of some sort. So it could have been self preservation, but it also could have been the guidance of my higher self. Something, some inner voice let me know that what the girls said would be so fun wasn't actually going to be fun, or a good idea. The still small voice gently guided me to go along with it, be cool, but keep my eyes and ears open. And if I was lucky, the girls wouldn't notice that I wasn't as stoned as they were. If I was lucky, they'd still let me be their friend.

After everyone but me was high as a kite, completely shit-faced actually, we all got into a car and planned to go to one of the girls boyfriend's apartment to keep the party going. Along the way the decision was made to steal gas from a gas station. This was in the days where you pumped first, then paid, so they wrapped a tee shirt around the license plate, pumped the gas and sped off. I remember sliding down the seat in the back of the car terrified we would get caught, or, even shot at. When we finally ended up at the boyfriends apartment, we stripped down to underwear and went night swimming. It almost seemed like things could be okay until one of the boyfriends pulled out a small sheet of blotter paper. I watched, wary, as all four of them dropped acid. The girls stuck out their tongues seductively to receive their doses, and then the boyfriend handed me a tiny white piece of paper. I'd played cool until then, and was ultra determined not to ingest this paper thing, so when they weren't watching I was able to drop the acid into the pool where I watched it disintegrate slowly. Things got progressively weirder, and in the wee hours of the morning, when my eyes were blurry from lack of sleep and I had experienced some of the most intense stomach and teeth clenching I had done in my entire short lived life, my brother and I tried not to watch the girls get naked with their boyfriends and continue having 'so much fun'. We sat, cold, exhausted, and unsure of how to act, where to look and what to say as we waited for them to take us home.

As a kid, I didn't yet understand these girls were not the type of people I should want in my tribe. I say this now with love in my heart for them, as the life they were living is all they knew. It was modeled before them, and, like all of us, they were doing the best that they could with the tools that they had.

The girls were seeking acceptance and connection, but were too young to know that neither would come from psychoactive drugs or meaningless sex. They were looking for inclusion, a chance to be part of something bigger than themselves. Ultimately, like all of us, they were just humans who wanted to be loved — and as for the ways in which they were going about it, well, it's what they were familiar with, and they simply didn't know any different.

I'm thankful that I later had the opportunity to live with different family members and friends who exposed me to alternate perspectives and lifestyles. Had I not, I may not have seen or known differently either. Though it reads now like I was disapproving that night, I went along with everything that happened, encouraging and participating in all of it (well most of it and as far as they knew- all of it).

Sadly, despite this experience with the girls, I still wasn't deterred from wanting desperately to be part of their circle. I still ached to belong. I obsessed over being liked. I needed to be needed. It wasn't the last wild night for me — I went on to have hundreds more experiences like this in my youth, sometimes as a follower, sometimes as a perpetrator. I kept playing the wild child cool girl through my teen years, even if it meant taking some risks and silencing my inner voice. Through my teen years, I continued to surround myself with people who were also desperately seeking love and acceptance in all the wrong places. Unaware, I kept building my tribe of energy vampires.

The pattern of choosing tribe members with less than ideal agendas, or good energy, continued for me well into my adult life. I continued to ride the wave of hanging with people who just seemed to bring me down to a less conscious version of myself. At the time I had zero awareness that my friends choices, the ones in which I considered myself "just along for the ride," were effectively blocking real connection and true love. I couldn't see that I'd hang with anyone because I was desperate to feel as if I belonged somewhere. I would do almost anything just to be included in the pack, because it was safer than going it alone.

Let me also state for the record that I was no saint. Be assured, plenty of times I was the defunct tribe member for others, having no regard for anyone or anything other than my own selfish needs. I have my own history of using others, abusing emotions and taking people for granted. Many times, I didn't bat an eye in making bad choices in order to feel as though I belonged, even when I knew the choices might hurt someone else or myself.

But. It is only because of these experiences that I have the compassion and empathy I do today for individuals making dangerous, hurtful and sad choices. Once we've gone through something personally, we're able to sit in non-judgement with people navigating the same struggle. Our trials and tribulations are what equip us to minister to or support someone else hurting through those same hurts.

Because of my own checkered past, I learned what vibes I definitely don't want to surround myself with, what to seek in a tribe member and how to discern true friendship. Maybe I had to learn the hard way, but I now value myself enough to be selective in choosing what people I will allow to have influence over me. Most importantly, I know exactly what type of tribe member I strive to be today.

If you are wondering, what in the hell a tribe even means, let me explain. A tribe is a circle of influence- a close group of individuals that matter to you, that influence you, that support you. When something goes awry in life, someone in this group is whom you turn to and who in turn has your back. When something is to be celebrated- it is this group who is the first ones with the champagne and balloons. When you f*ck up, this is the group who lovingly, yet boldly lets you know and then stands with you as you own it and move forward. A tribe may be fluid with individuals coming and going based on seasons and personal growth.

When we're lucky, we'll learn quickly that someone isn't a good fit for our tribe. They'll screw things up right from the get-go, throw dangerous drugs around, start physical fights for the fun of it, continuously drink and drive, participate in dangerous orgies, or obviously look for ways to undermine and belittle you. You'll know to run for the hills, and they give you easy excuses to do so. When we're not so lucky, or rather, when the universe has bigger lessons in store, the fact that someone is not the right tribe member may not be so glaringly obvious. Sometimes it's not immediately apparent. Sometimes the wrong tribe member looks like a best friend.

When I started my masters program, one of my dearest long time friends was in a place of deep, oppressive pain. In hindsight, I believe she may have always been there, but she came to a breaking point in her life with the pain she had been carrying and found herself spiraling downwards.

At the same time, I started a conscious awakening of my own, in which I saw how I was blocking love and connection. Clarity dawned on my attempts to control everything through lies, resistance, manic work and fear. As I learned to see the thought patterns and behaviors in me which limited my wellbeing, I was also being trained to discern mental health and behavioral issues in others through my school and residency programs. Out of misguided love, I made the mistake of trying to help 'fix' my friend.

Over a period of time, I set up trips for her to come stay with me for a week or more at a time (we lived in two different states) and planned all kinds of healing activities: volunteering at a shelter for abused women, attending church, taking yoga classes, practicing meditation. My efforts seemed futile as I watched her spiral further into pain. Each time she came to visit, the chasm between us seemed wider and it felt more difficult to really connect. During her final trip out to visit, I really felt a deep anger from her toward me.

I mentally exhausted myself trying to figure out the reason for her anger. Maybe she was resentful of my attempts to help? Maybe I wasn't offering her what she needed most — silence and space. Was I unknowingly hurting more than helping? Anxiety, guilt, and shame started to brew despite knowing I'd done every good thing I could think to do for her. I felt I'd failed, and I was bone-weary tired of trying. I struggled, trying to determine if my attempts at helping were misguided and my own desire to be needed was the primary motivator behind my actions.

Even after she left, heavy, draining, energy-sucking dialogue continued via negative texts, email messages and conversations. With each exchange or verbal encounter I was saddened by her determination to see the world as broken and out to get her. My anxiety about interacting with her was so severe that I got sick to my stomach when her number showed up on my screen. The sickness in my stomach turned to sadness in my heart. I was sad for her, but also for myself and the grief we shared in letting our friendship chart a different course. Because I knew, without a doubt, that the best thing for both of us was for our friendship to have a break, a hiatus. I wasn't the right friend for her, and she wasn't the right friend for me. Maybe not forever, but for then. We weren't serving each other's best interests, and it was time to gracefully acknowledge this and let go.

Signs you may have the wrong tribe (or tribe member):

» When you are with your friends and you are desperate to say something that will excite them or share something with the intent to feel included.

» When you are alone after spending time with your friends, you worry about what you said during the time with them.

» You carry nervous energy with your friends and are not really sure what is the right thing to say or do unless guided or directed by the friend(s).

» You feel the need to help or fix your friend(s) on a regular basis.

» After a conversation with a friend (or friends) you feel less than and unworthy.

» You get anxious and have to mentally prepare to visit with a friend (or friends).

Sometimes, it isn't just our immediate tribe of people we need to consider when it comes to what is influencing us. It is equally important to consider our energy, our spirit, and how to protect it. During my awakening, uncovering, and inner work which led me to realize my goals, one of the things which resonated most profoundly was the necessity of protecting my sacred energy. It is not only our immediate family, friends, and colleagues who influence our energy, but everyone we choose to engage with. In that respect, it's important to consider extracurricular activities, committees, and group dynamics, and how they affect the core of your being.

Case in point: mom groups. Some time ago, a good friend and I were discussing how we both stay away from many of the 'mom' groups because of the catty, gossipy, negative energy that often surrounds them. I told her that one of the biggest areas of focus in my life was surrounding myself with positive, upbeat, driven individuals, thereby protecting my energy. We are both overtly and subtly influenced by the people we engage with, so we discussed the importance of knowing what the energy was like of any group we choose to associate with. In simple terms, who you spend time with, you become like.

This isn't at all saying stay away from mom groups. There are beautiful individuals who are surviving major hardships and turmoil because of the support of incredible mom groups, who do great and wondrous works. It is a gentle reminder that we should evaluate the energy of any group or activity we decide to give our most precious resource to- *our time.*

This doesn't mean avoid all strife and pain either. If one of my tribe members was having a hard time, I would want to be the one that helps bring them back up (though not 'fixing' them). I would consciously and lovingly support them and help them to sort through their current pain and to aid them in the process of surrendering, trusting, aligning, and choosing love. But having a hard time is different than continuously seeing the world as broken, or being a victim, or gossiping, or criticizing, or judging. Continual behaviors reveal character, and surrounding ourselves with those of strong, noble character will fan the flames of those same qualities in ourselves.

Ultimately, in choosing who to surround yourself with, the intent of tribe members makes all the difference.

How to protect your energy:

> » **Don't invite everyone into your life.** Your mind, body, family, and home are all sacred places. They are not meant to be opened to anyone, anytime. This is not to say you shut the doors completely, but you take care and consideration into who you let in that will affect your thinking, your behavior or to influence you and your loved ones. It isn't necessary to close people off with a

stubborn and hateful heart, as you know that hurtful people are usually hurting themselves. Choose to not engage with them, and send love and healing thoughts their way. Just, you know... from the other side of the street.

» **You can't make everyone happy.** I used to have an especially hard time with this one. When I owned a few children's art studios in Dallas, I struggled constantly with the truth that I could not make every parent happy no matter what I did. It was debilitating until I just let it sink in: I CAN NOT MAKE EVERYONE HAPPY. Period. Other people's emotions are their responsibility, just as my emotions are mine. If I have heart centered, honest intentions in what I am doing, then I can rest peacefully knowing I am doing my best.

» **Don't feed it.** Recently, while waiting to pick up my daughter from dance at a local studio, I overheard a small group of moms talking. They were speaking horribly of other women, who probably thought they were friends. When one of those moms tried to turn to me to start a conversation, I literally got up and moved. Yes, yes I did. I work hard not to feed or allow that energy into my life. I have no intention of giving attention to people who want to speak poorly of others. Instead I sent her love for the pain she is carrying, and moved my seat. In my precious time here, I refuse to spend it talking badly about someone else, or listening to someone else talk shit. Guess what happens when you don't feed it? It goes away. They may talk about you now, sure, but do you really care? They would have either way, now you just won't know about the gossip. In this case, ignorance is pure bliss.

Sidebar: Can we talk about social media here again? My loving advice to you is this: Scroll less. Live more. In other words, get the fuck off of it. Yes, really. In today's western culture, most people spend a lot of time scrolling through social feeds, consuming carefully curated information about other people's lives and then comparing their own to the glossy, filtered images. I've seen people get upset about not being included in an event or gathering of 'friends,' which they never would have known about outside of social media. Though useful as a tool for business, and helpful for staying in touch, social media is a breeding ground for envy, fear, self-loathing, and anger, not to mention a drain on your time and energy. Though it can be a powerful connective tool when used mindfully, it can also be a tool for destruction. Marriages and friendships have been destroyed with the aid of social media. Wars, violence, death, political propaganda, the pain and suffering of the planet... these are all being prominently featured under the guise of 'news' and shared through social media. Be careful of what you allow in. If you spend time in that space of negativity, it plants a seed in you which may grow into a tangled vine of indignation, anger, frustration, or worthlessness. It also creates this very dangerous us vs them mentality. Cut out the root of the vine by cleaning up your feeds. If something stirs up negative thoughts or emotions, remove it immediately. Curate your social media accounts to make you feel good, because they are filled only with people, businesses, and campaigns that exude feel good energy.

Oh- and don't come back at me with, "Well, I have to know, I have to stay informed".

Here is what I will say back:

Why? What are you going to do with the negative energy you are getting from consuming this kind of information? Unless you plan to take compassionate and inspired action... Get. The. F*&#. Off. Of. It.

Do something else with your precious and valuable time. Turn to your child and hug them. Go outside and strike up a conversation with your retired neighbor. Go for a walk. Create art. Read a book. Spend more time in creation and connection than comparison and consumption. Your energy will thank you.

OK, that is all. You can return to posting in Facebook now.

» **Own it.** One of the important lessons I try to teach my kids is this: own your stuff. Be proud of the good, learn from the challenges, but own them both. When I make mistakes, I do my best to own them, and I honor that same effort in others. Recently, my dad called me to tell me he had lied to me about something small, but was big enough for him to feel the need to tell me about it. I was so proud of him because it is difficult to admit to lying, no matter the 'size' of it, it requires surmounting the fear that the receiver of the lie won't resent or hate you. But the truth creates freedom and expansion within, which is vital for peace and growth. When something less than ideal in your life happens, consider where you lay the blame. Avoid blaming others for your circumstances — after all, do you blame others when something good happens? When faced with difficulties, shortcomings or perceived failures: own them and move on. Blame, entitlement, self-righteousness; all of it leads to emptiness. Do your best to not allow others to blame you. If they do, see the second and third bullet here, and probably the first one.

» **Find your joyful place.** My joyful place is outside, with a breeze on my skin and the sun kissing my face. Sometimes it's in the breath and movement of a great yoga class, or the stillness and calm of sitting peacefully on my meditation cushion. Other times it's being curled up in the soft warmth of my bed, with a good book and a glass of wine. Find your happy place and go there when you need to. Don't look for happiness in other people — look for it in yourself first. Seek the joy that is your birthright, inherent in who you are and what you love.

» **Don't try to fix it.** It is totally ok for your tribe members to need a pick me up. As a friend or family member, that is what we provide to each other. However, if someone requires professional help or is in a space of desperate need, it is not your job to fix them. Intent here makes the difference. If the intention of your friend is to tell you about the challenge they are navigating in order to get re-aligned or uncover their own resolution through external processing (talking), then grab a glass of wine, sit down, listen and hold space for them. If the intention is to gossip, criticize or take someone down, lovingly set your boundary. Grab your glass and hit the road, sending love and good vibes from afar.

My prayer/ask of the universe:

Thank you for the guidance and ability to openly and gracefully discern the energy surrounding me. Thank you for giving me a heart to receive the best in others. Allow me to be a source of love for others and to seek the same in those I surround myself with.

Questions to ponder:

If you think about your five closest friends- do they project the attributes you want to be known for?

_____

_____

Describe what attributes are important to you (and consider if you display them yourself). Examples: trustworthy, humorous, generous, open hearted, bold, driven, altruistic...

_____

_____

You become like the closest five people you surround yourself with. Look around you - is that what you want? - **Shannon Jamail**

PART 3

Align

Stories

The one thing that you have that nobody else has is you. Your voice, your mind, your story, your vision. So write and draw and build and play and dance and live as only you can. - **Neil Gaiman**

When I was thirteen years old, my aunt and uncle invited me into their home to live with them. They lovingly, graciously welcomed me into their hearts, and, you know, wallets, because raising a teenager is not cheap. They made major life adjustments, uprooted their family and my two younger cousins, and willingly moved to a new home just to accommodate the responsibility of my guardianship. When I reflect on the chaotic mess I was at that time, I am deeply humbled that they took me in. Such generosity speaks volumes to the vastness of their hearts, and their love and support still fills my heart and gives me strength today.

During the time that I lived with them, they introduced me to something that I still love today — the vast magnificence of the wild desert. In their care I experienced camping under the dark expanse of starry skies, fireside chats, the simple pleasures of time spent outdoors. They exposed me to adrenaline pumping adventures on quads, ATVs, and motocross, and to this day the smell of gas from revved up engines transports me back to fond memories of wild times in the wilderness. The stories I recall from that time have shaped and formed a big part of who I am today.

One day, during a desert trip, my uncle took me and one of my cousins out for a late day motocross ride. Tearing through the desert, wind in our hair, my cousin and I were amped in the way that only youth experiencing the thrill of danger can be: hungry, bold, and full of fierce faith that we were impervious to danger. We were untouchable and indestructible, free-wheeling dirt demons stirring up clouds of dust as we roared through the desert on our bikes. At the conclusion of our last ride, my four year old cousin asked his dad if he would "please please please" let us go around again. It was almost dusk. Anyone that knows about the desert knows that you don't ride at night, unless you are lit up like a Christmas tree, because dark in the desert is DARK. My uncle looked at me, visually assigning me authority, and said, "Make sure you stay behind him and only do one more loop." He trusted me with my fierce, wild independence and the bravado of my youth.

As my cousin and I took off, I remember being overcome by the most intense sense of freedom. All the ugliness, violence, drugs, and instability in my life leading up to that point faded away as I felt, in that moment, so totally *free*. I remember the wind whipping across my face and sunset painting fiery colors across the sky, red fading to purple as night fell on the beauty of the desert which unfolded before me. In that palpable freedom, possibility expanded, and I felt a deep surety that everything was going to be alright - maybe even better than alright. Maybe even great.

In that magic moment of freedom, I gunned the bike and let the wind blow my hair wild, the cool air kissing my arms and face, the sound of the engine empowering me to speed up, turn harder, ride faster. I was entranced and enchanted. And then... then I was totally and completely fucked. I lost my cousin. My four year old cousin, to whom I'd been assigned responsibility, was nowhere to be seen. He'd vanished, and I was the only one to blame. I was devastated, wracked with guilt and overwhelmed at how quickly I had managed to make a good situation go bad.

It took a huge search and rescue team over five hours to find my four year old cousin out in the dark, cold, predator infested desert. By the grace of God, they found him huddled up against his bike, which had run out of gas, trying to stay warm, and trying to stay *alive*. Then, and now, I think of the countless ways in which he could have died that night, and how every single one of them would have been my fault. The trauma of that experience instilled in me a deep story that I felt I must always carry caution in my back pocket, and never feel too free, because the world could come crashing down around me in any moment.

From that night until even the present day, I have carried with me the ability to turn on a dime from feeling incredibly blessed and free to haunted by doom and fear. I've held onto a single proverbial shoe - and I'm always waiting for the other shoe to drop. When things are going swimmingly and my life feels amazing, I immediately look for what may be lost, what could go wrong, how I could have screwed it all up.

Search for what's messed up and you will almost always find it, because the universe responds to our vibration. When my vibration is high and free, the universe responds in kind, and when my vibe is doom and gloom, the universe gives them right back to me.

We have the capacity to achieve greatness simply by *believing* we can, by aligning our vibration with clear, inspired intention and elevated emotion. What we focus on expands, and when we choose to focus on the magical, synchronistic, positive aspects of our lives, those grow. Unfortunately, many people don't subscribe to this concept and even fewer step out in faith and use it. We also have the capacity to achieve loss, destruction and limitations simply by believing in them as well. When we focus on hardship, lack, negativity, they expand into ever widening black holes which draw us into our own decline. This mindset of negativity *is* used by most people, though we often don't realize it. *Side note: This isn't to say that only bad things happen when we are in a bad place. Sometimes bad things happen to teach and shape us. To aid us in elevation. To open us up in ways we wouldn't have without the experience.*

In my teen years and early twenties I believed (unknowingly) that I would only be worthy of love and acceptance once I could buy and have nice things. I spent much of my childhood poor. Like the kind of poor where our car didn't have reverse — when we had a car. We were evicted more than times than I can count. I believe I moved at least twelve times within twelve years but can't be sure I didn't forget a few. I remember standing in the free lunch food line at school, waiting for my friends to finish their lunch and praying they would have extra on

81

their plate to throw away (why did it always feel like the free lunch tray had less damn french fries than the paid ones?). Casually, I'd mention that I would eat it for them.

I mostly traveled back and forth, from state to state, parent to parent, with a few pit stops with other family members and friends. One parent wasn't as destitute, but when I lived with the other, which was most of the time till my high school years, we were broke ass poor. I watched this parent struggle desperately with bills, evictions, broken cars, juggling my sibling and I along with work, living with other family members and friends and eating spam as a luxury meal. If you haven't had fried spam, with miracle whip, on white soft bread you haven't lived.

To say it was tough, especially for my parent, is an understatement, but during those years of difficulties I was also forming key beliefs in and about myself. Amongst the chaos, I was writing an internal narrative that reared up as an adult — one that I unknowingly lived by despite my own eventual successes.

When I started working at the age of fifteen I immediately recognized the pure pleasure of having money and became addicted to the surge it gave me each time I could look at something and then own it. I bought all the things I never could have before, including items I had only seen in magazines or on TV. As I bought things, I imagined that I became more likable, more desirable, just *more*.

Even around the age of twelve, I was already consumed with this idea that the things I had were my worth. I secretly bought jeans at a swap meet, carefully removed the fake triangle name brand and stitched on the Guess emblem so, well, that no one would notice (remember when they were the bomb jeans?) because that was only way I felt accepted, with labels and brands and status symbols.

As I got older and worked, I was actually able to buy name brands... so I did. The story weaving itself within me was, "I am loved because I have nice things." Inward variations of the same story, I told myself: "I feel good because I can buy these things, I am important because I can buy these things, and I am secure because I can buy these things."

Nice things are nice, but they are not love, health, importance, or security, and they most certainly are not self-worth.

This story didn't change until my late twenties, when I surrendered my six figure (twice over) corporate job and went to no job. During this time, I moved out of my comfortable beautiful home in Southern California into a new state, with no friends, no job, no income and no prospects. It took a shock to my 'identity' — the surrender of my corporate job and cushion life — to realize that it wasn't the money, or lack thereof, that defined whether or not people liked me, or if I belonged. My value and belonging had nothing to do with the car I drove or the house I lived in. And, if to some people those things did matter, then that wasn't a person I wanted to like me anyhow, because we gain and we lose all external influences. Nothing outside of us is really within our control. What really matters, and what my story finally became is: "I have so much to offer, the world- and all of it is *inside* of me."

Our stories, the internal narratives we weave both consciously and unconsciously, affect us all. Sometimes stories arise from specific events (like losing my cousin in the desert) and other times they are created by a gradual buildup, a collective of individual experiences, observations and influences. These stories become deeply ingrained and habitual, thought patterns set on repeat in our minds.

Consider the way social media has impacted the way these mental stories unfold, lighting up insecurities and fears in countless people. Often, as stated in the chapter on comparison, we tend to view someone's highlight reel on social media and compare it to our editing scraps on the floor. We create mini stories in our head, that may (or may not) be based on long standing ingrained stories that confirm insecurities, fire up anger or incite indignation. As social media proliferates, more studies are becoming available on the negative (and positive) impacts that social media networks have on users. One of the underlying emotions most often cited as being triggered by social media usage is envy.

One of the common stories most of my clients experience, and one I have also struggled with, is the feeling of being less than — of not being enough. This story can show up in all aspects of our lives; our romantic relationships, families, careers, and social lives.

Recognizing you may be stuck in your stories:

» You lie or make up things so that your story is different.
» You feel fear when you think of a limiting belief or story that has come up time and time again.
» You want things to be different but don't know how to change them.
» You constantly look to others and compare.
» You simply believe that something, even if desired, is just not in your deck of cards.

When I first started writing this book (or a version of it) several years ago, I kept stopping. I found myself falling into the story of, "I am not a good enough writer." It went something like this: "My life isn't special enough. I don't have enough wisdom, experience, knowledge, or inspiration. I am not as good as so-and-so." When this story reared it's ugly head, I put the manuscript away, told myself to go back to 'what I do best' and tried to forget it. Despite quitting many times, I felt a persistent, continuous calling in my heart. "You need to write this out," my inner spirit gently reminded me. "It isn't about so and so, it is about you, and you are not writing this for the glory of being a writer, but to share and connect and grow."

Truth be told, right now, I have no idea how many copies will sell (my husband may buy a shit ton, so there is that). I don't know if the message will connect, or if I *am* inspiring enough. But I am writing it anyway. I am choosing to rewrite my story. I am showing up, and showing up is my super power. I am visualizing myself sitting on Oprah's chair in her yard discussing it. I am loving myself in the process. And whatever the result — it will be perfect. I believe this in my core. Because I am growing, learning and transforming myself in re-writing this story — literally and figuratively.

How to change your story:

» **Awareness.** The first step in changing a limiting belief or story is to recognize it.

» **Thank your story.** Essentially fear (the basis of limiting beliefs or stories) is really intended to be a protective force field, so thank your past story and let the story know it is no longer needed.

» **Create a mantra.** Next step is to replace it with a mantra or an affirmation, like "I AM good enough and am becoming the best version of myself every day."

» **Confirmation.** Look for evidence to support your new story; "I am good enough because..."

» **Utilize visualization:** *I see myself doing XYZ because I am good enough.* You can visualize mentally, keep a journal or use a vision board.

» **Mediate and pray about your new story.** Ask for guidance. Ask for strength. Seek love and offer love within your new story.

» **Love yourself through the process.** It is easy to get started, then get frustrated and be hard on yourself. Offer grace and love, and start again.

Important note: Throughout this book we talk and dig into some painful and terrifying aspects of our lives. If you find yourself stuck in a dark place, seek professional help. Trauma, grief, anxiety, depression and more are not something to be ashamed of or feel that it is an inside secret job. Help is available. Please know — help is available — and you are too valuable to not seek it. Find some important information on this in our resources section at the end of this book.

My prayer/ask of the universe:

Thank you for my past stories and beliefs for their intended protection. Thank you to these stories for shaping me to where I am now. I no longer need these stories and am releasing them. I am open and embracing the truth and empowerment of my new stories.

Questions to ponder:

What evidence is there to support your new story(ies)?

_____

_____

_____

_____

What mantra or affirmation best supports your new story(ies)?

_____

_____

_____

_____

Power & Perspective

Definition of a victim: a person to whom life happens. - **Peter McWilliams**

Psychologists have said that memory retention begins in children around three to five years of age. If the first memory is traumatic, retention may begin earlier rather than later. The first memory I retained is from when I was around three years old. In many ways, it feels as fresh as when it happened. I still can smell it, hear it, feel it.

The wailing sirens approaching through the night echoed the sound of my mother's screams, increasing in volume as events inside the house spiraled out of control. Suddenly, flashing red and blue lights appeared, adding to the chaos and confusion all around me. From my hiding spot in the bushes, the earthy smell of fresh cut grass filled my nostrils. I heard the sound of my name being called, over and over, as the police and my aunt searched for me. Paralyzed, I stayed right where I was. My heart pounded inside my chest and hot tears streamed down my face as certainty filled me that my mother was dead. Sitting in the bushes, I could hear my name being called in the distance, see the lights dancing through the leaves, but I was stuck in a loop, unable to move, replaying in my head the images of my mother being chased by my stepfather with a recently sharpened ax. Her screams were vibrating in my mind. My brain was stuck on repeat, replaying over and over what had just transpired: My aunt waking me up and telling me in a frantic voice to follow her as she ran out of my room with my baby brother in her arms. Climbing out of bed and sliding on slippery socks into the kitchen where I froze and couldn't move despite my aunt still shouting at me to follow her as she ran out of the front door. Frozen in place, watching as my stepfather came hurtling through the house and past me with a large, red-handled ax above his head, monstrous, his fiery eyes filled with rage. I stayed there, frozen, until I heard my mothers screams. Their shrill intensity rocked my body, releasing my paralysis, and I stumbled outside as fast as my legs would take me. My aunt was nowhere to be found. I was alone and terrified, so I hid.

This is my first memory. I can still replay it in vivid light, sound, and color. Memories created before this time, and for a significant period after, are a bit blurry and out of order until about five or six years old, but this particular memory is indelibly marked, imprinted permanently, stitched forever into my memory bank.

Trauma and negative encounters create lasting neural pathways in our brains, from which we later weave recurring internal stories related to them. Trauma informed neural pathways and thought patterns often create a cycle of triggers and negative feelings. These hard wired pathways affect our emotions and resulting actions, and often create recurring thought and behavior cycles which simultaneously drain us of joy and fill us with fear.

Humans are biologically predisposed to sensing and perceiving stress and danger in the surrounding environment. The fight or flight response, also called hyper-arousal, is a physiological reaction, a protective system that occurs in response to a perceived harmful event, attack, or threat to survival. As humans, our brains and bodies are constantly searching for danger. Even if we don't have traumatic stories of our own, we can find or create them based on our surroundings. In prehistoric days, this mechanism was a necessary biological adaptation based on life or death environmental stimuli. It was "eat or be eaten," and the acute stress response of fight or flight enabled the human nervous system to navigate perils like being hunted by a saber tooth tiger.

Thousands of centuries have passed, but the same wiring is there, now it is drawn to other 'dangers' which present themselves in our lives. Often they appear as newsworthy topics such as terrorism, racism, socioeconomic distortions and so forth. We are physiologically inclined to participate in the stress and fear. We are drawn to it, physically and emotionally, and many stay there, addicted to the adrenaline and other neurotransmitters which are stimulated by absorbing the perceived threats. It's easy to operate in that space and refuse to turn just a little further and notice what else is happening in the world, what else is available, what else we are capable of.

Repeated and prolonged exposure to the fight or flight response, prompts some people to stay in a mental state surrounded by negative memories, emotions or even current actions and say, "I can't function because of... (my past, my trauma, my pain, oppression, that person, something someone else did, etc.)" This cycle only serves to creates victims. People become victims of their perspective, their belief system, or their stories.

It is so easy to blame circumstances or past trauma for current fear, anxiety, reluctance, or failures. We often hear people lay fault or blame for their current circumstances on a variety of external factors uninvolved in the present situation. Examples might be:

- "I suck at relationships because of my childhood, my parents split up when I was little."
- "I didn't get the job because the hiring manager is racist."
- "Yeah, I got fired, but not because of me. No one could do that job, it's too hard."
- "I didn't get picked for the committee because no one likes me."

You get the idea. Instead of looking within, blame is placed on the past, societal factors, other people, or anything other than internal causes and personal responsibility.

Before I proceed further on this topic, let me first say that I lived in this victim mindset for longer than I am now living outside of it. I relished blaming anything or anyone — my past, my coworkers, my boss, my friends, the government, the waiter, the traffic, my computer, my phone, my curling iron — for my problems. Nothing was my fault, everything was someone else's fault, and I always found ways to justify this. Because, funnily enough, there are some nuggets of truth in our thinking which align with the blame we place. This is what confuses and misdirects us. It's true, the traffic was terrible, making me late to work. My phone did unexpectedly die, preventing me from following up on a call. My co-worker was an asshole, making work an unpleasant place to be.

The problem with blame is that despite sometimes carrying a seed of truth, it fails to take into consideration of the most important and powerful determining factor in your happiness - you.

By staying in the blame game and victimhood, we relinquish power. We relinquish the ability to choose different thought patterns and behaviors, and thus stay in the cycle of hell and chaos. We even unwittingly create more of the circumstances we don't want by thinking about them, talking about them, and focusing on them. By saying, believing and thinking about our negative circumstances, we literally create more negative circumstances. We remain stuck while we continue to complain and replay negativity. We become sad, depressed, defensive and lost in self-pity as we affirm the perspective that the world is out to get us.

Signs you may be operating in blame or victimhood:

» Your boss doesn't appreciate you.

» Your friends don't return calls or texts.

» Your kids don't respect you.

» Your parents weren't loving or supportive enough.

» Your health is failing due to genetics, poor medical attention, or lack of healthcare availability.

» Your finances are suffering because you are not paid what you are worth.

» You feel used, abused, neglected and rejected.

Does any of this sound like you? If so, let me add my name to the list of jerks in your life and tell it to you straight:

You are making yourself a victim. Everything you are thinking and feeling is your fault. Own your life. Own your thoughts and feelings. They are yours — not your bosses, your spouses, your friends, your parents, or your kids — yours. And that is great. It is great because now you know, and you can do something to change it. YOU. Not *them*.

Surrender to your power instead of surrendering to victimhood.

Many people stay in the space of being a victim because of fear or recurring mental stories; many people are afraid to change because it is more comfortable to operate in the familiar. Sometimes victimhood even feels right, satisfying in it's own way, and people respond with sympathy to our plights.

Sympathy, however, is usually short lived as people get tired of the complaints and powerless mentality (unless they are victims too, in which case you will play the 'who's problem or blame is bigger' game). Feelings of affirmation, justification and comfort of staying in a space of victimhood are usually part of a story the ego has created in an attempt to protect us from danger in the unknown.

One of the most common examples of the mental stories crafted by the ego is that of blaming our environment or the "nurture" factor for our actions, behaviors, or life circumstances. I won't go into the nature versus nurture debate, as there are many studies available that do that already, but I will share some information from a powerful study discussed in one of my psychology classes years ago. This study was another one of the reasons I decided to continue my education and pursue a psychology degree at the masters level, as it revealed to me my own habitual blaming of others. The study suggests (as do many neuroscientists) that a parent's job is almost done the day they leave the hospital, citing genetics as the dominant factor in shaping personality. The study draws the conclusion that more than half of our collective differences come from genes rather than the way we are raised. Twin studies refined this suggestion, including one which an example is drawn from below.

Does the preference for a clean environment come from genetics or upbringing? One set of twins were separated at birth and adopted by two different sets of parents. When they were interviewed at twenty-seven years old, having had no contact at all with each other since birth, both were concluded to be obsessive-compulsive neat freaks. When asked what drove this behavior, both blamed their adoptive parents. One twin said that it was because his adoptive parents were slobs and he didn't want to be a slob like them. The other twin said it was because his adoptive parents were very neat and clean, so he made sure he was always neat to please them.

It is suggested that no matter what household they would have grown up in, they were destined to be 'neat freaks' simply by the genetic coding within them.

What does this mean? It means that although you may choose to use the victim language here and say, "See, I am screwed because my parents gave me jacked up genes," you could instead empower yourself and say, "I now know that I am capable of changing my thoughts, emotions and behaviors and align them with what is good and feels good which have nothing to do with my past experiences. I know I have the power to change."

Side note: my intention is not to get people fired up here on the importance of raising our kids in a healthy nurturing environment. That is a given. This is not a case for bad parenting, abuse or neglect. It is an example to aid us in eliminating our past or childhood experiences as the 'reason' we are f'ed up. Ok, moving on.

What happens if you don't change? What happens if you stay in the blame game and the state of victimhood? Nothing happens. You stay there. Do you get relief by holding on to the blame? Do you get back at the other person(s) by holding on to this perspective? No. Blame, and the accompanying emotions of anger and bitterness, are self-defeating.

Employing blame as a tool for dealing with a situation is is like drinking poison and hoping someone else dies (remember that from earlier?).

We have the power. No matter who your parents are, where you live, what ethnicity you are, how much money you have, what religion you were brought up in, what mistakes you have made thus far, how straight your teeth are… you can change your outlook. No matter your circumstances, you can choose a different perspective. An important note: changing your perspective doesn't change the circumstances. Rather, it changes how you view them, in turn changing how you feel, and finally changing how you act.

Here's an example: Driving down the road, I am blindsided by another driver merging into my lane who comes inches from my bumper and almost causes a serious accident. Panic courses through me, adrenaline surges and I defensively yell out angry curse words - almost. Then I stop and consider the situation: I am unhurt, my car was not hit, all is well. Most likely, the near collision was unintentional, as people do not usually try to get into car accidents.

Now, changing my perspective isn't going to change the fact that I was almost run off the road by a driver, but it can change the way I respond. By assuming the driver didn't see me, or considering the possibility that they had an emergency, and then wishing safety and well being for that driver (and gratitude that I wasn't hurt either), I am able to change how I feel. Changing how I feel also changes my subsequent emotions and determines my next set of actions. Instead of chasing the driver down, flipping them off and then carrying the anger and anxiousness in me, which I later will transfer into my next encounter with my kids, spouse, client or friend, I will carry peace and well being instead. As *A Course In Miracles* suggests, a shift in perspective is quite simply a miracle. We have the ability to create miracles, every day.

A significant portion of my childhood was a shit show of violence, drugs, racism, abuse and poverty. I can't change that. I spent a near equal portion of my life blaming my shortcomings and failures on my history, experiences or lack of XYZ. Today, instead of spending more time blaming my past or the events of my childhood for what I have or don't have, I have deep gratitude for the way in which adversity shaped my character, instilling in me values of compassion, non-judgement, humility, and empathy. I am able to understand that everyone did the best they could with the tools that they had, just as I do each day. I can see that my family loved me totally and completely in the best way they knew how. Today, I am able to recognize there was true beauty and love weaved throughout my whole childhood that I had chosen to ignore by focusing on blame and pain.

Another side note: Often we expect to be loved the way we want to be loved, instead of meeting people where they are in their love style and ability. By recognizing it may be different than the way we give or receive love, we will experience more peace, connection and acceptance.

Because of the challenges I have experienced, today I am better equipped to do what I love than if I hadn't had the experiences at all. The tribulations of my past have softened me to sit in compassion with people struggling through some of life's darkest difficulties.

By emphasizing the importance of cultivating internal peace while facing external challenges, I should note that I am not suggesting you ignore racism, abuse, neglect, or any other social conflict, or stay involved with individuals who hurt you. Make any changes you need to in order to be safe so you can do the internal work. Positively educate yourself (this means not by the news stations or social platforms) and compassionately fight for what you believe is right.

Move from blame to self-empowerment. Examine your perspective about what you have experienced and work to make positive changes in your mentality by approaching experiences and circumstances from a victor, love-based approach — not a victim, angry or fear based-approach.

Why is this important? If you want to experience joy and fulfillment, you *must* change from victim and powerless to victor and powerful. No victim will truly be happy. No victim will live up to their full potential.

None. I don't know one person, that is happy, joyful and at peace, that blames anyone for anything. Do you?

Steps to surrender to power:

» **Acknowledge your current victim based mindset** and thank the past stories for their 'protection' while also dismissing them. Let them know you no longer need their 'protection' and that you are taking on a new way of thinking.

» **Acknowledge that you do have the POWER to choose** your thoughts, your emotions, and your actions and that you can only change YOU, which is all you need.

» **Take a look at your tribe** and ensure you have the right team in place to uphold your new beliefs.

» **Read books, listen to podcasts**, watch shows that support your new belief system. Some of my favorites which I re-read, re-listen, re-watch:
   • *Law of Attraction*, Esther & Abraham Hicks
   • *The Jess Lively Show* (podcast)
   • *Think and Grow Rich* by Napoleon Hill
   • *Seat of the Soul* by Gary Zukav
   • *The Four Agreements* by Don Miguel Ruiz
   • *Oprah Winfrey's Super Soul Sundays* (podcast)

» **Learn a way to stop** when you feel yourself become defensive or are ready to blame. My friend April loves to say out loud to negativity, "Cancel! Cancel! Cancel!" Whether it is this, or a visual stop sign, start a programming in yourself to STOP the process and then flip the script to empowering words.

» **Pick something you want to respond differently to and practice it.** For example, in the road rage scenario I described: Instead of getting upset, take some deep belly breaths, put an upbeat song on, listen to a great podcast, smile at yourself in the mirror, etc.

» **Get rid of the BUTS.** When you apologize, or respond to someone — don't follow it with BUT (an excuse or opportunity to blame something or someone else). Simply apologize or respond.

» **Create a personal mantra and/or practice affirmations.** Put up post it notes, record yourself saying them and listen to them several times a day. I live by this mantra: Change begins with *me*.

» **Choose empowering language.** Language shapes thoughts, emotions, and behaviors. Choose positive language even before you believe it. For example, if you are ill, then say, "I am getting better and healthier every day." Instead of talking about the symptoms, speak aloud instead about how healthy you are getting.

» **Ask yourself: How can I view this in love?** In all things we can find a more loving, less blaming way to view it. It just takes practice. One way I do that is by looking at something and saying to myself, "What would I tell someone *else* about this situation, pretending it is theirs and not mine?" This helps us to remove attachment to the situation in order to view things with more clarity. Viewing things in love also means to offer grace to ourselves. I still find victim thoughts popping up in my head. I simply forgive myself, repeat my mantra and forcefully change my thoughts.

My prayer/ask of the universe:

Please soften my heart toward those that have or are hurting me. Please allow me to embrace that hurt people, hurt people and that I have the power to release anything that is holding me down or causing me suffering. Empower me to shape my own reality by owning my thoughts, words, and actions. Thank you for the courage and strength to choose to look at these situations in love.

Questions to ponder:

Think of someone or something you are currently blaming for a perceived short-coming. How can you look at it in love?

Who within your tribe demonstrates the ability to be a victor versus a victim? What can you learn from them?

Abundance

> *Whatever we are waiting for - peace of mind, contentment, grace, the inner awareness of simple abundance - it will surely come to us, but only when we are ready to receive it with an open and grateful heart.*
> **- Sarah Ban Breathnach**

Somewhere around late 2007 or early 2008, my husband and I were teetering dangerously on the brink of bankruptcy. We had used up both of our savings accounts and my 401K, a sum approaching a million dollars, in order to build new businesses over the previous three years. We were down to our last few thousand dollars in the bank, and our financial situation felt more dismal than it ever had since we'd been married. I was anxious, discouraged, and fearful that the hard work and finances we'd poured into our businesses may not be recouped. It seemed like time to pull back from any unnecessary spending and be more cautious than ever with our money.

As we sat in church one Sunday, I looked at my husband and asked him, "Do you think should we stop tithing until we figure out what we are going to do?" This was a loaded and surprising question in our relationship, as I was the one who had insisted we tithe in the first place, whereas my husband had not been a big believer in giving any organization our hard earned money.

"Good idea," I thought he would say, "we could use that money to pay our mortgage this month."

But he didn't say that.

"No," he said, "as a matter of fact I think we should increase it. I think we should tithe ten percent of what we *want* to earn. We have to believe it to see it."

I was absolutely floored by his willingness to press further, to lean into discomfort and trust fully in the blessings that were ahead.

After I pulled myself up off of the floor, I remember feeling an intense release, a beautiful surrender inside. I started laughing, almost uncontrollably.

"I am in!" I said, "I have been broke ass before, I am not afraid to be broke ass again."

Despite my flippancy and joking about losing it all, the truth was I felt expansion and freedom in that moment. The sensation and perception was of a freedom to *receive*. The tension, fear, and intense fight for control dissipated and I felt myself resting in the peace of surrender.

As I shared earlier from Carl Jung- what we resist persists. When we resist the current circumstances and cultivate fear and aggression in fighting for control, we create more of what we don't want. When you truly surrender what you think you need or want, what you really need (and want) shows up.

Right after we left church that day, our circumstances began to change dramatically. I mean, it seriously was less than twenty four hours later that we received the first unexpected business opportunity. From giving out of lack, and surrendering to divine will, our entire world shifted. More business opportunities came in within a month period than we had seen in the entire previous year. Our finances soared and over the next few years we ended up increasing our tithing again and again, as we kept surpassing what we *wanted* to earn. Don't get lost in my words: this isn't about tithing to a church, but about surrender and opening up to receive.

It is important to note though, that in order to receive, you do have to give. We have said this before: the universe abides in reciprocity. Whatever you want, you must first give it. If you want love, you must show love to others. If you want peace, you must act peacefully in your thoughts, words, and actions. If you want abundant finances, you must be willing and open with your financial generosity. A warning and word to the wise: This principle operates the same way with negative qualities. If you give hate, stress or judgment, the universe will reciprocate those as well. Choose your frequency wisely.

How to recognize you are blocking abundance:

» You continuously seek and speak about the things that are going wrong in your life

» You think about and talk about the debt you have (even when you are talking about "reducing debt" you are still talking about debt)

» You speak from a problem based perspective vs a solution based perspective

» You expect bad things to happen, bills to be in the mail, bad news to be delivered in a call, email or letter

» You expect people to cheat you, double cross you or lie to you

About six months before I got serious about writing this book, my husband and I found ourselves in yet another seemingly serious, somewhat ominous financial situation. Being self employed, even after twelve years, doesn't come without its blessings, and blessings often come disguised as challenges. This blessing in disguise came after my husband Nathan experienced some serious physical injuries that left him physically and emotionally crippled for an extended period of time. With his energy and focus being challenged, he was unable to work at the pace we were accustomed to, and we found ourselves quickly running through our savings again.

As the money dwindled, that old nasty fear began to root and grow in our hearts, and the natural response was to try to seize control of the situation. Heated, anxious discussions of bankruptcy, selling the house, and taking out loans took place late at night, while the kids were asleep. We immediately defaulted to our old way of thinking, believing that by controlling or resisting the current crisis, we could force it to turn around. One morning, after several months of being in this stage of resistance and fear, I woke up super early, before anyone else in the house. From my box of sacred items, I got out my sage, then lit it and walked the house while setting my intentions. Sitting in the quiet of my home office, I burned my abundance candle and did a deep meditation. Covering all my bases, down on my knees I prayed and asked for guidance.

The response to my penitence and energy work? Nothing. Silence. The universe, God, was failing to respond - and I'd done everything right! I did what I was supposed to do! Now where the hell was my answer?! I raged and cried and then lay on the floor, spent.

"Surrender."

A calm, quiet, authoritative voice spoke within me. A second passed as I sat with this internal command, considering what do to.

"Surrender."

Down to my knees I returned, hot tears streaming down my cheeks.

"Please allow my heart to soften and open," I prayed. *"Please* allow my mind to be eased, and for my control to be released. *Please* allow me to show up, to trust, to surrender. Thank you for the incredible abundance that I currently have, and that is continuously, effortlessly coming my way."

In the stillness of the early morning, on the floor of my home office, my words seem to almost reverberate, flooding the space with their truth. It was not the magic of the words themselves, but the spirit they contained, one of humble surrender, gratitude, and trust that I would be provided for. Surrender is hard to describe, but we know it completely when we feel it, when the walls have finally broken down and we are laid bare before something greater than ourselves.

I picked myself up off the floor and again, like at church eight years earlier, I felt a huge sense of release. I scuttled up to my desk, grabbed my journal and started feverishly writing. Words poured from pen to page and as I wrote, I realized what I had been missing was not only surrender, and trust, but alignment.

Moved by an unseen force, I started writing out everything that felt good. Words stacked upon each other as I continued, writing everything that aligned with love. The pen flew over the page for minutes and then fell to the side, spent. I gazed at my journal and read through the soul download of what feeds, heals, and renews my spirit. After looking at the list I realized some life changes were going to be in store. I needed to take inspired action based on aligning myself with what felt good and right.

Keep in mind, at this point, my husband and I were not in a place to reduce income, yet this is one of the inspired changes that came forth. Well, not to reduce income, but to work smarter rather than harder. To do less so that I could focus more. It meant eliminating some programs I was currently offering, reducing my client load, and refocusing my efforts, career wise, on just a handful of specific projects. By doing so, I'd create space to align my family and personal focus on creating more joy, laughter and love.

Insert fireworks here.

After I walked out of my home office, it was like butterflies were alive in me. I wasn't worried about whether we would have to file bankruptcy (who cares?) or whether we'd lose our house (so what!). All I wanted to do was be love, see love, create love and surrender the rest to my higher source, trusting that everything would work out perfectly, as it should.

It did.

And boy, did it. Within twenty-four hours we got a random check for nearly five thousand dollars in the mail. It was from our mortgage company, we had overpaid on our property taxes. Less than forty-eight hours after that we were notified by our accountant that we were going to be getting a refund of almost nine thousand dollars. We had overpaid our income taxes, and I gotta stop here, because anyone that is self employed knows this shit is almost impossible. For the last twelve years we have literally received a big bill that we owed, not the other way around. This was a sure sign that it was a greater force at work than coincidence.

Less than a week after that I got a text from the person who had bought my chain of children's art studios a few years earlier. His text said that he was going to be mailing me a check, the payoff on the owner financing we had arranged with him. He still owed two years of payments, but he wanted to pay early. Out of nowhere, he was sending a very large check to us fulfilling the balance of his loan debt.

Within thirty days of my surrender, my husband and I collected over fifty thousand dollars of unexpected money and despite decreasing my workload, I was pulling in more money with less work.

What. The. F*%#.

I don't want to give the impression that abundance is exclusively about money. During both of these situations, I also received more love, compassion, and grace than ever before. I developed a stronger bond with my husband. I created the craziest most wonderful memories with my children. I found connection with family that had been missing.

Abundance isn't about money. Or cars. Or houses. Or clothes. Maybe shoes. Ok, not shoes.

Abundance is about finding your proverbial cup overflowing. It's about experiencing gratitude for all that you do have, recognizing the blessings in your life, and honoring them. Abundance is also about alignment, and alignment starts with surrendering.

How to surrender to abundance:

» **Surrender** to your higher source.

» **Trust** that you will be taken care of, no matter what that looks like. It may or may not require a change in address. It may or may not require a change of jobs. Regardless, the end result is always, will always- be perfect.

» **Find gratitude**. It can be difficult to find the things we are grateful for when we are surrounded by fear and chaos. Take the time to write it out. Send thanks and appreciation for each and every thing you are grateful for, from the very breath you take, to your warm blanket at night. Write thank you notes to God, to the Universe, to your neighbor, to your parents, to co-workers. Spend all of your free time, not on social media, but sending gratitude and appreciation out. You can't expect to receive more when you are not grateful for what you currently have, no matter what that looks like.

» **Align.** Nothing good happens when we are out of alignment. The old adage, like attracts like, is a universal truth, and when we are feeling like shit, it is shit we will attract. Find joy, humor, laughter and love. Don't surround yourself with negative nay-sayers. Create affirmations. Watch funny movies. Read inspiring books. Listen to uplifting podcasts and music. Don't allow yourself, for one moment, to give away your joy because of someone else's words or actions.

My prayer/ask of the universe:

Please allow my heart to soften and open, for my mind to be eased, and for my control to be released. *Please* allow me to show up, to trust, to surrender. Thank you for the incredible abundance that I currently have, and the abundance that is continuously, effortlessly coming my way.

Questions to ponder:

What can you give that you also are seeking?

_____

_____

_____

In what ways can you surrender to abundance?

_____

_____

_____

Stress & Anxiety

> *The greatest weapon against stress is our ability to choose one thought over another.* - **William James**

I haven't wanted to commit suicide, but I have most certainly wanted to die.

When I was about fifteen years old, I began to have severe trouble with fear and anxiety, especially at night. I'm talking about the not able to breathe properly, hard to swallow kind of fear. It especially arose whenever I considered what happens after we die, though sometimes anxiety would just come on up and try to get cozy with me for no apparent reason at all. Crippling anxiety still tries to be my best friend, decades later.

Despite the intense fear of dying, there have been times in my life where death would have been *welcomed*. Not in the sense that I would want to aid it, but rather that death would be a great relief, because living was just too damn hard. I've experienced prolonged moments where the infinite unknown, the gaping abyss of blackness beyond name, form, space, and time, beckoned me with a siren song, because it would give me rest from the overwhelming panic and fear in the present moment.

Sound extreme? Yes, well, this is what anxiety looks like for me.

A large reason I went to school for a masters degree in behavioral health sciences was because I was determined to find a solution to my anxiety. I didn't want to treat it, I wanted to *cure* it, permanently. I was convinced that diving deeper into psychology would equip me with tools and tricks to overcome, crush and completely eradicate anxiety from my life.

I learned a lot in school. Like, *a lot*. I am so grateful for the education, experience, residency and clients that allowed me to figure out what the f*&k anxiety is, how it manifests and ways it can be treated.

However.

Anxiety can't be cured. It can't be crushed. And despite my conviction and desire, it cannot be entirely eradicated.

Anxiety can, however, be embraced. I can surrender to it in order to grow and learn from it. With mindfulness and coping tools, I can learn to skillfully dance with my anxiety in order to live joyfully *with* it.

That is not what you wanted to hear, right?

Yes, I know. I totally understand. It isn't what I was seeking either.

How to recognize you are suffering from stress or anxiety:

» *1st- if you are concerned about your stress or anxiety- please seek professional help (see the list available in our resources or contact your doctor).*
» If you experience physical symptoms such as grinding, gritting teeth constantly
» If you have trouble sleeping at night with ruminating thoughts/worries
» If you are experiencing other health problems such as digestive issues, high blood pressure, unusual weight gain/loss
» If you feel alone, lost and overwhelmed more often than not

I grew up surrounded by mental health crises. My immediate family has a history of schizophrenia, depression, bipolar disorder, general anxiety disorder and a big heaping scoop of addiction. I saw first hand how painful, debilitating and often deadly mental health disorders can be. Are genetics a component? Sure. But perhaps even more influential than chromosomes are beliefs, perceptions and mindsets about mental health. What we think about mental health often shapes how, when, or if it will affect us.

Important note: there are very deep and powerful mental health disorders that are affecting millions of people. They are not something I take lightly and, anytime one is feeling hopeless, desperate or wanting to give up- seek professional help. There are specific therapeutic tools and yes, medications, that are available that are not discussed in this book. Please check our resources pages at the end of this book with some links and contacts.

I believed, from a young age, that I would suffer as I saw my family suffer, and suffer I did. Was my suffering a result of genetics, or did it manifest because I continually put it out in the universe that I expected it? Possibly both. Maybe it is written in my DNA, or perhaps it came to fruition from my thoughts alone. A definitive answer may never be found.

Regardless, what has allowed me to move past the pain and daily, exhausting-as-hell suffering is believing that I can also embrace it in order to transcend it. Not numb it. Not deny it. Not fight it. As I have mentioned several times already, "What we resist, persists."

Embracing anxiety may sound impossible if you're in the midst of it. Aside from learning to dance with your suffering, there are a bounty of preventative tools and practical measures which can aid in relieving anxiety and stress. Nutrition, physical activity, meditation, cognitive behavioral interventions, prayer, and medication are a few of the tools which help many people prevent anxiety episodes and/or navigate them more gracefully.

This book isn't about nutrition or physical activity. I don't teach a specific way to move or eat, though I do believe that what you consume, and how you maintain your physical health are important. The wise and all knowing Google, and a knowledgable holistic naturopath can help you figure out what you should eat and how you should move your body for optimal health.

This book isn't about meditation or prayer, though I believe they are crucial components to our overall health. There are amazing books and digital platforms on meditations, prayer and spiritual awakening that can completely transform your life.

This book isn't a diagnostic or treatment manual for the cognitive behavioral guru seekers. There are millions of books for that too and even more professionals available to help

This book isn't about medication. I'm neutral towards medicating for anxiety and recognize that at times, for some people, it can be a great tool to serve a specific purpose.

This book isn't going to teach you how to eat, exercise, meditate or medicate your anxiety away.

This book is to tell you to stop fighting it. Stop numbing it. Stop running from it. Stop denying it.

This book is to tell you to show up, face to face, with your anxiety and embrace it, surrender to it so you can learn and grow from it. So that you can transform from it into your highest potential.

Embracing and surrendering doesn't mean playing the victim. It doesn't mean you can use your 'anxiety' or 'stress' card to be rude, unkind or unloving. It doesn't mean you can use it to run away and hide either.

Embracing and surrendering means being curious. It means searching your thoughts and emotions to ask: *Why are you feeling this way and how can you align in a higher vibration?*

There is scientific proof now that stress and anxiety cause a plethora of physical ailments: Heart disease, high blood pressure, diabetes, strokes, auto immune disorders, digestion issues, muscle tension, insomnia, depression... the list of afflictions goes on ad nauseam. The number one cause of doctor visits in the United States today is stress related health concerns, cited as a contributing factor in over ninety percent of appointments across medical disciplines.

If it's so common, and most people with access to healthcare today are experiencing stress related issues, what is the root cause of such widespread stress and anxiety? Where is this epidemic of stress coming from?

Here is the thing: Most human stress and anxiety comes from fear. Please note, I understand some physical and genetic exceptions exist, but even in those circumstances, fear exacerbates the underlying causal factors and enables stress and anxiety to flourish. Fear is the root.

And fear, put very simply, is a lack of love.

Consider this example: You are stressed out about not meeting a deadline at work.

Stressor/Anxiety Trigger: Work. Deadlines. Work load. Expectations.

Be curious. Why are you feeling this way? I am really worried that I can't do what is expected, that it is too much.

What is the real fear? That I am not enough.

Fear root: Fear of being fundamentally inadequate, unloved, and unappreciated.

Isolating and exploring the root of stress or anxiety can bring to light fear roots, but this alone doesn't stop the cycle of anxiety or halt stress in its tracks.

What is the rest of the answer then? It isn't simply to take a pill, or visit a therapist for the rest of our lives (though, if that makes you feel good, and isn't an escape, do it). It isn't to numb out with drugs and alcohol, or look for acceptance and love in sex and dangerous relationships.

What is the rest of the answer to experiencing less stress and anxiety overall?

It is to align in a higher vibration and return to love.

How do we do this? This part is the easiest and hardest part of this entire book.

Do what brings your soul, your inner being- joy.

The more you align yourself in joy, in activities, people and circumstances that bring you joy, the more aligned you are to receive and participate in more things that bring you joy. What we focus on, expands. As you experience more joy and less fear, you'll find yourself experiencing more self-love, and more love in the world around you. Also, and this is very important — when we focus on *self love*, acceptance, forgiveness — our relationships with people and the world around us changes. Everything becomes brighter, lighter, softer.

This isn't to say that other activities such as therapy, meditation, high vibe nutrition, physical exercise, healthy boundaries, breath work and other mindful choices don't aid in our overall well being. On the contrary, all of these components are powerful tools for wellness and healing. But doing any of these activities, without also seeking alignment, will not provide the peace, freedom and total physical ease you are capable of feeling.

I want to clarify something right away about embracing and surrendering. It never means to sit idly by, waiting for the universe to bring you what you desire. That is not surrender, my friends, that is laziness. Embracing and surrendering means surrendering to the idea that when you align in love and joy, and take inspired action, you can detach from the outcome of the entire process, because the outcome will be perfect no matter what.

This is what happened when my husband and I were on the brink of bankruptcy we discussed in previous chapters. Even if we lost our house, our cars, all of our savings- it would have been perfect *still*. The outcome didn't matter, only our intentions and our inspired action mattered.

Important side note. Stress and anxious feelings/thoughts are not the same as a mental health diagnosis of GAD or other anxiety related disorder. Those struggling with a diagnosis of a mental health disorder can absolutely still benefit from the meaning, point and thoughts in this chapter. But I also encourage you to find a professional that can lovingly support your journey to embracing who you are on your way to self-love and acceptance. Check out the resources at the end of this book for more information.

How do we align in order to dispel stress and anxiety:

» **Embrace it.** Make peace with it. Understand, that like in our chapter about fear, we can choose to look at it as if the intention was to protect us. Thank it for the protection that it is intended to provide.

» **Nourish your temple, your body.** Feed it, move it, love it in the best possible way for you.

» **Align yourself in your highest vibration.** List out what brings you joy and make choices to be in that state as much as possible.

» **What you focus on, you manifest.** Don't talk about your stress unless it is with a solution focus mindset. Don't talk about your backache, or high blood pressure, or anxious thoughts, unless it is to say how healthy you are becoming each day. Force your eyes, your thoughts, your entire being toward health, prosperity, joy.

» **Choose love.** In everything you encounter, including stress and anxiety, ask yourself: How can I see this in love?

Embracing our stress and anxiety means surrendering, trusting, aligning and choosing love.

My prayer/ask of the universe:

Allow me to embrace what I am feeling today and surrender to it in love. Thank you that I can choose to raise my vibration in order to align in joy.

Questions to ponder:

What brings you joy?

Examples:

Bubble baths
Glass of chardonnay
Kombucha in a pretty, sparkly glass
Hiking
Reading
Masturbation
Running
Long hot showers
Talking with high vibration friends
Swimming
Boating
Traveling
Knitting
High heeled shoes

Yoga
Praying

_____

_____

_____

What is the root cause of my biggest stressor or anxious thought?

_____

_____

_____

Anxiety and stress are not my friends, nor my enemies. They are gateways to my highest vibration. - **Shannon Jamail**

PART 4

Choose love

Truth

Truth: I am a recovering liar.

In my time upon this earth, I have lied about big and small things. I've lied about things of great importance, and things that didn't matter at all. I've lied to my friends, my family, and myself. When I tried to come up with specific examples about lying for this book, I became overwhelmed because, sadly, I have lied about so many things. I've put Pinocchio to shame with the extent of my untruths. Thankfully, his story isn't mine, or I'd be up to my ears in bills from the plastic surgeon for my nose jobs.

Here's the thing: By lying, I created a web of bondage which prevented me from the peace and understanding that is only available through telling the truth. You know the old adage, "the truth will set you free?" It's a cliche for a reason. Lies create burdens and suffering within us, oppressive spiritual heaviness which weighs us down and keeps us captive. Telling the truth allows this weight to be lifted off of us, removing the burden and inspiring a huge sigh of relief at the surprising lightness of our own being.

My lies, as many lies do, stem from my fears, insecurities, and shame. I remember the first time I was the subject of someone else's lie. I was in kindergarten and the teacher was very strict about not interrupting circle time. I really had to go to the bathroom (I am sure I waited too long... I was five) and as I was walking to her circle time group to ask her if I could go, she gave me the sternest, scariest look and pointed to my desk. I went back to my desk and squirmed, shook and then, unable to control myself any longer, peed in the chair. I was ashamed and humiliated.

The school called my mother to bring me new clothes and as I stood there, trying to explain to my mom what happened, the teacher looked right at my mother and lied through her teeth.

"Shannon never even asked to go to the bathroom," she said. "She never even got up, she just sat there and peed." I clearly remember thinking, *Wow, adults lie?* I was incredulous, stunned, and the chagrin of that moment combined with the revelation of human fallibility burned itself into my memory.

Still today, I can clearly see everyone's face, feel the temperature of the hallway, the coldness of my wet pants, and the disappointed stares. In retrospect, I know that my teacher lied because she knew she had done something wrong. By refusing my advance, she was neglectful of my needs, and rather than acknowledge her mistake, she chose to lie instead.

One of the first times I can remember being caught in a lie, I was around seven years old. I had an accident, again, sort of. Basically, I didn't wipe well after using the toilet and ruined a pair of underwear. I know, I know, too much information, but please give me a free pass because it's in the interest of truth telling. I hid the skid-marked underwear beneath my bed at my then stepmothers house. She inevitably found them and when she asked me about them, I lied. I was afraid and ashamed, and lying seemed to be the best course of action to avoid getting in trouble. It didn't go well, though, as I ended up with a bloody nose, my father yelling and my step mother accusing, blaming, and shaming me in her disgust. I remember thinking, not that I needed to tell the truth in the future, but that I needed to do a better job of getting rid of the evidence.

The underlying trend here isn't that I may have had bathroom issues as a child, but that lying became an intrinsic part of my story and life from a very young age. I would like to stand on the righteous podium of "I lie, not to deceive or hurt, but to protect or enhance myself," but the truth is this: a lie is a lie and is hurtful no matter what. It causes pain, even if only to myself. Which it does, by the way, every single time. Lying hurts my self worth, self confidence, and self image. *Lying harms my energy and ability to truly connect with others.* It is impossible to fully connect with someone, to love or be loved, when that connection is built on lies, no matter how small or 'white.'

Humans are remarkably intuitive creatures, and lies are always felt, even if not overtly evident or known. This concept is something I didn't understand until my mid to late twenties. Think about this for a moment: When you are with someone and they talk to you about something, can you sense the genuineness or truth behind it? Can you also sense when something is off, even if you're not sure what it is? As good as I became at lying, we are never good enough to deceive one's inner spirit or intuition. Lies build glass walls around us that we are constantly checking for cracks. They drag us down into perpetual worry that the walls will shatter down around us. Operating in a world of lies is exhausting, scary and lonely.

Looking back, one of the common threads was that I usually lied to create an emotion I desired to feel, or avoid an emotion I found threatening. This manifested in multiple ways: exaggerating things so I felt included or awed others; eliminating information to avoid punishment, trouble, or looking bad; or blatantly lying in order to create humor, love, or acceptance.

Sometimes it's lies of omission. For the past sixteen years, I have led people to believe different things about the father of my children. Or, I should say, fathers. I have three baby daddies. Three fathers, four children. I have allowed people to assume, without correction, that all of my children are from my current husband. Though, if you look at our family pictures, you can clearly see the United Nations going on with everyone being part Italian mutt (me), part Filipino, part Pakistani, and part Lebanese. I've also let people assume, without correction, that I was married before and that the older two are from my ex-husband.

Here is the truth:

I had my first baby with a boyfriend at nineteen. This child, my firstborn son, has grown into a handsome, courageous, funny, outgoing man: in his twenties now and married to a gorgeous woman. They're about to have a baby... I'm gonna be a nonna!

My second kiddo came when I was twenty-six. I wasn't married to her dad, either. She is my tenacious daughter who is so kind spirited, relentless in her pursuits and has a compassion for the world.

I had two more daughters with my current, and only husband, one at thirty-two and one at thirty-five. Both are lively, spirited little firecrackers. One is incredibly thoughtful and so driven we have to jump out of her way. The other is a free-spirited creative dreamer, wild and carefree.

I choose to allow these assumptions about my children's parentage, or in some cases, straight out lied, in order to hide my shame. I lied to cover my insecurities, so I would not have to see judgment reflected back in the eyes of others. I believed that if people knew the truth, it would give them permission to judge me.

This fear sometimes seemed validated when the truth actually did slip out. Years ago, when my then fiancé, now husband, introduced me to his family, and was explaining my first two children's parentage, one of his family members told him (with loving intent, but lack of grace), "I probably wouldn't tell everyone about all her baby daddies".

Open the floodgates of pain and shame. That experience, and others like it, led me to conclude that it was easiest to simply allow people to assume a single father for all my kids, or maybe a previous marriage. But I learned to never volunteer the truth, because condemnation was sure to follow.

The problem with this is — lies still hurt. And even though the judgement of others is painful, denying the truth is even more painful.

You may be struggling with truth if:

» You tell lies and sometimes are not even sure why you are lying.

» You feel a strong need or urge to expand a story to be liked or fit in.

» You fear rejection if you tell the truth in certain situations.

» You constantly feel left out unless you make up stories or activities.

As a child and young teen, my recurring lies were a way to include and elevate myself so that others would want to be in my presence. In my mind I was pretty damn special and hip, I just needed more sparkles for others to see it. When I lived with my mom in Ohio, I would tell people how amazing things were with my dad in California. I spun tales about how we always went to Disneyland, the beach, and saw celebrities in Los Angeles. I wove an elaborate fantasy that we lived in a big house and that I had all the name brands and newest cool stuff at his house. When I lived with my dad in California, I would tell people that I got to do whatever I wanted in Ohio, that my mom was so cool she would let me smoke (well, actually she did) and get tattoos (wait, she did that too.) I spun things however I could to make me look like a worldly, mature, experienced hippie living a cool life. The problem was, most of it was not real. Though parts of what I said were true, the message was false. I was only trying to create an image of myself that other people would be impressed with, regardless of how far it was from the truth.

In order for me to stop lying, I had to learn to love and embrace myself. I had to accept that my life isn't meant to be more or less than what I have experienced, done, have, or am. I had to accept that mistakes are okay, and that being quiet, or having nothing to contribute other than holding space, is not boring or lame. When we lie, we are effectively blocking anyone else from the opportunity to accept us and love us *as we are.*

What did I find when I stopped lying?

Peace. Stillness. Love. Acceptance. Freedom.

> *I found peace in knowing that I wouldn't be 'found out' and in embracing the truth of who I was.*

> *I found stillness in my mind- no more worried chatter or planning on how to keep up the lies.*

> *I found love for the real, raw, imperfectly perfect version of myself.*

> *I found true and beautiful acceptance in real friendships and relationships.*

> *I felt free to be completely me. Only me. Not anyone else or a pretend more sparkly me.*

Our truth, no matter how ugly, boring, annoying or embarrassing it may seem, is always more inspiring and relatable than any lie.

How to surrender to the truth:

» **Practice.** This may sound silly to someone reading this that may not have a problem with lying, but practice telling the truth. When the urge to lie hits you (and it is an urge first no matter how minuscule,) choose the truth or choose to be quiet. Then choose it again. And again. If you slip up and lie- recognize it quickly, be bold in admitting the lie and sharing the truth instead. You may be surprised how humility and honesty will be received with grace when you acknowledge your lie right away.

» **Choose to love yourself first**. When you want to lie about something regarding your life, body, relationship, job, kids, bank account, or any other aspect of your life — stop and silently say the truth in a beautiful, loving way. Affirm that you are worthy exactly the way you are. You are enough.

» **Forgive yourself**. There is nothing but harm in rehashing what you have lied about in the past. If you find certain things need forgiveness, pray and meditate about it and perhaps ask for it (though don't feel as if you need it in order to move on). Otherwise, leave it where it is — behind you. Forgive, learn, grow, and transform.

My prayer/ask of the universe:

Please allow me to see myself with love, and release all fear, shame, and insecurities which tempt me to lie. Thank you for guiding my thoughts and words to the truth and feeling confident and peaceful in that space.

Questions to ponder:

Think of the last time you lied (or wanted to lie.) What was it about, and why did you feel that way?

_____

_____

_____

_____

Practice writing the opposite of the lie above (the truth) in a loving and supportive way:

_____

_____

_____

love

When I was around fourteen years old, a thirty-five year old man, recently released from prison, tried to forcefully have sex with me. He had me trapped in a back bedroom, easy prey for his forcible advances. He was aggressive, but thankfully the ramshackle house had thin enough walls that the people getting high in the living room and kitchen would be able to hear us if I screamed. He was just scared enough of going back to prison that he backed off when I resisted, and I was able to get away.

As I ran off, I knew his behavior was deeply wrong, but I was so conflicted by what I had witnessed and experienced over the last decade that everything was getting mixed up. At fourteen, this wasn't the first time I was assaulted by some man who thought it was his right to come after me.

My perspective on sex and love was a jumble of thoughts which ranged from confusing to terrifying. On one hand, I knew that sex and violence didn't equate to love or acceptance, but on the other hand that is precisely what I had been subjected to, witnessed and 'told' by the adults around me.

I once watched a family member hold a knife to his wife's throat as he made her sit naked and watch television. Although she cried quiet and desperate tears, she also shimmied up to him when he said certain things to her, despite him having just pulled her hair and smacked her head around. Their marriage was one of my early examples of 'love.'

129

My brother and I would go to prisons (yes, plural) with my mom to visit her newest pen-pal-turned-boyfriend and watch them swap spit. The make-out sessions were a cover for physically (via mouth) swapping of a twenty dollar bill. If you haven't heard of, or better yet witnessed women bringing men money in prisons and exchanging it via tongue swapping... well, my friend, you haven't lived.

Because she believed that these convicts loved her, I watched my mother do this time and time again — willingly giving her affection and money to those who regarded her as disposable. Time and time again, I watched her get pissed off because the convicts dumped her when she didn't have enough extra cash to bring in her mouth. To my young, malleable mind, the message was this: you are worthy of love only when you have something to give: sex, money, material goods.

I watched the women in my life use sex as a tool, a bartering chip, and a weapon. I learned that affection was transactional, conditional, unpredictable and volatile. In the relationships of the most trusted adults around me, women were routinely physically and sexually abused — all with the word love thrown into the mix.

This was a big part of my introduction to love.

Needless to say, I had some reframing to do.

Currently I am studying *A Course in Miracles*, which is considered a guide to spiritual transformation. It is at minimum a year long course, but truthfully, it is a *lifetime* course, as is everything we are attempting to achieve. I don't believe there will ever be a time that I will experience *complete* peace, *complete* love, *complete* surrender in *complete* continuity until I am spirit again and walking in the presence of the divine.

Though I don't believe I can embody perfect, unconditional love in this lifetime, it doesn't stop me from trying. With each day, each moment, we have the opportunity to experience love, not as an emotion, but as an action. Love is something we can actively choose to do — it is a verb, and it is a choice.

As I am studying, living, learning and transforming, there is one guiding principle, other than surrendering, that I am inviting into every thought, word and action: *Choose love*. Real love. Not the kind of love that ends in painful, desperate whispered promises over broken bones, battered bodies and bruised faces. Nor the kind that is penned in cajoling, manipulative letters from imprisoned strangers who have committed heinous crimes and now live without even the possibility of parole. The love I'm choosing isn't the one muttered about by lost, lonely souls with glassed over eyes collecting needles, baggies, and pills with a greedy, aching need. And it's not the kind that comes with strings and expectations, quid pro quo and tit for tats.

The word love has become diluted as we twist it to meet the needs of a broken world, but beyond our human shortcomings there is a deep, abiding kind of love which remains steadfast, pure, redemptive and healing.

It is this greater kind of love that says, 'we are connected, we are one, we are all broken, we are all healed, we are all together.' Life is a series of lessons, composed of both hardships and triumphs, strung together to draw us ever deeper into understanding the breadth and truth of this great love. Life, then, is not about mastering fear, but about mastering love.

I want to set the record straight — my goal in life is not to be happy, because happiness is elusive and temporal and has been confused with a state of being versus an emotion. My goal is not to acquire or obtain material things, because everything external can be taken away or lost (although I do love a good pair of shoes and yoga pants). My goal is not to be famous, recognized, and known, because that, too, is fleeting and ultimately meaningless. My goal is to love: to be love, to receive love, and give love- in thought, word, and deed.

If mastery of love is the pinnacle of human achievement, and being love is the apex of our evolution as divine beings of stardust trapped temporarily inside these meat suits, then intentionally, continually choosing love is the highest ambition to which we can aspire.

Choosing love is our ultimate goal.

Choice is, by definition, mutually exclusive. This means that there is always an alternative action which we must reject in order to choose love. Choosing love means rejecting fear, transcending envy, denying bitterness, and refusing malice. Love is the replacement verb for every action which does not align with the highest good of yourself and others.

Part of choosing love is rejecting comparison. When we get into weeds of comparison and competition, we lose... always. Even if we think we 'won' (my house is bigger, my marriage is happier), we lose, because we have lost our ability to connect and recognize the sameness in another person. A dear friend of mine once said, "Competition and comparison are not real, only personal excellence is real. How can we measure one person's excellence against another's? If we operate in excellence, then competition is no longer necessary and comparison is futile." I love this. There is no standardization for success in life, as every experience is ultimately subjective. Rather than measuring ourselves against others, we can simply check in with whether we are excelling to our greatest capacity; when we are, it doesn't matter one bit what someone else is doing.

Choosing love also means refusing martyrdom. We can't truly love or be of service, unless we are safe, secure, and provided for in our own basic needs. Because of this truth, it is vital to align ourselves before we reach out to others. Like the announcement on airplanes, put your own oxygen mask on first before you help your kids (or husbands). What is best for you is best for everyone around you, as long as the alignment starts in love. Too often, particularly with women, we relate choosing love to self-denial, to neglecting our own needs, and to putting ourselves last. This is a fundamentally flawed operational strategy! When we are anxious, fearful, hungry, and drained, we cannot serve or love others. Tend to your own needs first, and you will find your cup overflowing so that you can pour love into others.

When we choose love, we reject judgment. As Mother Teresa aptly put it, "If you judge people, you have no time to love them." Too often, we project our own judgments, insecurities and belief systems onto others. We may even go so far as to confuse judgment with love, offering condemnation under the guise of concern as we proclaim to care only about 'what's best for them'. Judgment and love cannot co-exist, because in order to judge someone, we have to make them wrong. Judgment entails correcting, convincing, controlling, or changing people, and makes blaming, complaining, and condemning permissible. When we stop trying to change others, we gain the opportunity to love them *as they are,* which teaches us empathy and compassion, two of the fundamental building blocks of real love.

Choosing love does not equate to seeking it. This may sound counter intuitive, so allow me to explain. If we are out of alignment, love-seeking is the expression of a desperate need to fill a void that is impossible for another human to fill. The wellspring of love is internal, not external. Failure to realize this leads humans to look for love in all the wrong places. Love-seeking and the desire to be cared for can also cause us to respond to situations based on how others will think of us versus how we actually feel. Sadly, it causes us to also seek approval and connection from sources that are disconnected from love completely.

A client I just started working with continuously finds herself in a pattern of seeking love in all the wrong places, with all the wrong men. When she notices someone she finds attractive, she unconsciously tries to change herself to fit their desires and preferences. If they love sports, she loves sports. They drink beer, she drinks beer. If they are a rock music lover, then hell, so is she! She became a shapeshifter of the soul, and in doing so, every time, she loses herself.

Changing herself for men meant emptying herself of all the things which made her authentically her. This leaves her feeling desperate, lonely, and hollow inside. The relationships, built on lies, never work out either. Each time, she eventually tires of pretending to be someone she isn't, and grows weary of feeling lost. With each guy, she inevitably moves on, looking for the next person who might be able to fill the void within her.

I'd like to disclaim here that I'm not denying the potential to find connection with other people through romantic love. On the contrary, true, deep, abiding romance is one of the deepest sources of connection we can experience in this lifetime, but it's seldom born of desperate seeking. It is born first, of loving oneself and then having an abundance of genuine love to offer to others.

Though the circumstances leading to love will be different for everyone, one thing that holds true: lasting, real love requires a wellspring which starts within. Love yourself first, and then extend that love to others.

One of the greatest ways we can actively choose love is by watching our language. Language is a powerhouse, a force to be reckoned with; It is the gateway from thought to vibration, and alignment to action.

If thoughts start in love, but the words come out in complaint form, then the love stops and everything after results in disconnection. Words can be destructive or constructive. They can elevate, exhort, encourage, and empower, acting as a buoy for the human spirit, or they can criticize, complain, correct and control, dragging spirit down to the depths of despair. In Buddhism, a teaching exists to apply three criterion to your words before you speak: Is it true? Is it necessary? Is it kind? Unless you can answer yes to all three, it may be better to remain silent.

Take a moment to reflect, to think back on the course of your life. What words have been spoken over you which retained so much power that you've continued to believe them? Do you remember the cruelest thing ever said to you? Most of us do. Here's the real challenge: Do you remember the kindest? The weight of our words is so powerful, especially the negative ones. They sear themselves into our memories, creating scorched earth where beauty and love struggle to grow. So when you choose your language, consider carefully: will these words harm, or heal?

I'll dare to tell you one thing that can change your entire existence. This magic bullet can turn you towards love quicker than any other activity you could do. Are you ready for this?

Stop complaining. Stop complaining about the weather, your spouse, the kids, your dog, your friends, parents or childhood. The more you complain, the more the universe will provide you things to complain about. The more you complain, the more you are blocking love. Complaining drops you back into that victim place (remember that?). Words are *powerful*.

Here's a cognitive behavior activity to help curb complaining that I adapted from Will Bowens *A Complaint Free World*:

- Start by placing a bracelet on one wrist. Pick a bracelet that is sturdy, because this practice might take a while, and your bracelet might see some wear and tear.
- The goal is to keep it on the same wrist for 21 days straight. This sounds easy, right? If you complain, judge, criticize or gossip, you have to move the bracelet to the other wrist. Every. Single. Time. And start over on day one.

Still sound easy? Maybe for you. For me, it took over six months to do it. What I learned from this is that learning to choose my words carefully is not a one-time deal, it's a lifelong practice.

Like choosing my words, choosing love is also not an achievement to be won. It, too, is a lifelong practice. When I say my goal is to live in love, it is not just about the "big" things like my marriage and parenting. I aim to choose love in every detail of my life, in the big and small decisions alike, in my thoughts, words, and actions.

> *"Beauty is when you can appreciate yourself. When you love yourself, that is when you're the most beautiful."* - **Zoe Kravitz**

There isn't a magic formula to figure out if you are choosing love, but there are some universal truths that may help guide the way.

Universal truths to choose love:

» Release expectations for people to react or respond to you in a certain way.

» Meet people wherever they are on their journey, without correction, condemnation, or judgment.

» Choose to forgive. This doesn't mean to be a doormat, but forgive to release your *own* suffering.

» Give people the benefit of the doubt. Look for the best of *everyone*, and leave the rest with grace.

» Realize that you cannot choose love in your own power alone, the ego prevents it. Align with your inner guide and spirit, asking it to choose love for you when you are unable.

» When making decisions, strip away money and other people as contributing factors. Make your decision as if money weren't an obstacle and your decision wouldn't hurt anyone else.

» When making decisions, identify and strip away limiting beliefs about yourself. Ask yourself, "What do I fear? What if that fear were not real?"

> *"Eventually you will come to realize that love heals everything, and love is all there is."* - **Gary Zukav**

Learning to choose love requires forming a habit. It is something to practice daily, hour by hour, minute by minute. It is that simple, and it is that difficult. Choosing love means learning to overcome our old stories and learning to let the inner spirit guide us, rather than the ego. It means learning to harness the power of our language and perspective, learning to be still and live in truth. To choose love, we must learn to receive abundance, release fear and embrace pain.

To master choosing love, we must practice not only when it's easy, or when we believe someone is deserving of our love, but in the circumstances where loving is most challenging. It is easy to choose love when someone or something aligns with our beliefs. That doesn't take much effort on our part. When we love people or situations which deserve our love least, this is the testament to the power of choosing love. This is where we build character and strength, within and around us. Loving in opposition unites us across barriers and boundaries of faith, politics, skin color, sexual preference or gender identification. Choosing love, together, is how we win.

> *"Love one another. As I have loved you, so you must love one another."* - **Jesus Christ**

Choosing love of our own accord is impossible without aligning with our inner spirit. To choose love, we must also learn to surrender to the divine which exists in all and through all. Love is our natural state and our birthright, but we must consciously seek to remove the obstacles we build that prevent love from operating. To choose love, we must surrender to love.

My prayer/ask of the universe:

Please guide my thoughts and alignment to love. Allow me to see everyone as a connection to myself. Thank you for allowing me to surrender to love.

Questions to ponder:

In what ways are you blocking love or seeking it in the wrong places?

_____

_____

_____

In what ways are you choosing love?

_____

_____

_____

> *Success isn't measured by what you have, but by how often you are aligned in love.* - **Shannon Jamail**

Fulfillment

Afterward

Only those who have learned the power of sincere and selfless contribution experience life's deepest joy: true fulfillment. - **Tony Robbins**

I just got home from a rare personal night away. I travel frequently for business, but the last few years have not held many personal nights away. This weekend I not only got away, but had the best day planned — a spiritual growth workshop in Los Angeles, dinner with a group of like minded spiritual seekers and then a slumber party at a hotel with the editor of this book. So many great things happened during this brief but bountiful, twenty four hour escape. I laughed so hard I almost peed and my cheeks hurt from genuine joy. I was moved to tears several times with little 'a-ha' nuggets. My editor, who is also my friend, shared that she sincerely felt this book will be a light to readers as it has been for her working on it. Umm... Does it count if I pay her to say this? Yeah, it totally counts!

Despite it being an overall wonderful experience, I was reminded that it is all just part of the journey. We attended a workshop on detoxing from judgment, during which I reverted into a darker place and judged too many times to count. Maybe it was simply the subject matter highlighting awareness of my shortcoming. Maybe I was feeling a tad insecure about the upcoming dinner with some powerhouse spiritual seekers. Maybe it was just because I was being an asshole. Whatever the reason, I didn't beat myself up for it. I acknowledged and surrendered to it. I offered myself grace from it while trusting that there is a higher power at work that is trying to show and teach me something. I then sent up a silent prayer and choose to consciously send love to those whom I had judged.

Life is a cycle of seasons. It is a continual return to grace. It is a living, breathing, moving energy mass that includes making mistakes and then dusting ourselves off and returning to surrender, trust, alignment and choosing love again, and again, and again.

This book isn't meant to be a cure for anything. It isn't meant to hold life's answers or to be a road map to success.

It is a glimpse into one person's journey to fulfillment. The definition of fulfillment is 'the achievement of something one desires' and my desire was, and is, to return to love. That is where you will find me.

What is your desire? Love? Acceptance? Connection? Abundance? Well, my dear new friend, the only thing needed to attain your own fulfillment is for you to take just one tiny step. Just one step, then maybe another. Start with one. And that first one is simply to surrender.

Thank you, from the depth of my heart and soul, for investing this time in you and in us, as a connected and sacred human species. My prayer is for your journey to be filled with all that you desire and that your fulfillment reaches every inch, cell, and atom of your being.

Resources

National Suicide Prevention Lifeline - 1-800-273-8255

Substance Abuse and Mental Health Services Administration (SAMHSA) Treatment Referral Helpline- 1-800-662-HELP (4357)

Anxiety and Depression Association of America: https://adaa.org

Depression and Bipolar Alliance: www.dbsalliance.org

Mental Health America: http://www.mentalhealthamerica.net

National Alliance on Mental Illness: https://www.nami.org

Help for service members and their families: http://www.mentalhealth.gov/get-help/veterans/index.html.

Find more tools and links as well as downloads and meditations at: www.mindbodycomplete.com/surrender

Notes

Notes

....
....
....
....
....
....
....
....
....
....
....
....
....
....
....
....
....
....
....
....

Notes

Notes

Notes

Notes

Notes